Love to
Mary
from Lelah
& Bob

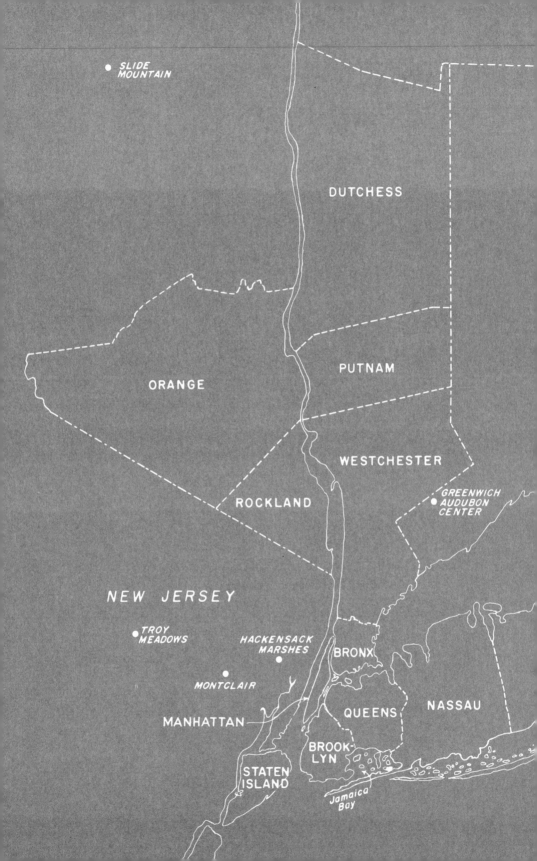

AREA COVERED BY THIS BOOK
[see pages 55~124]

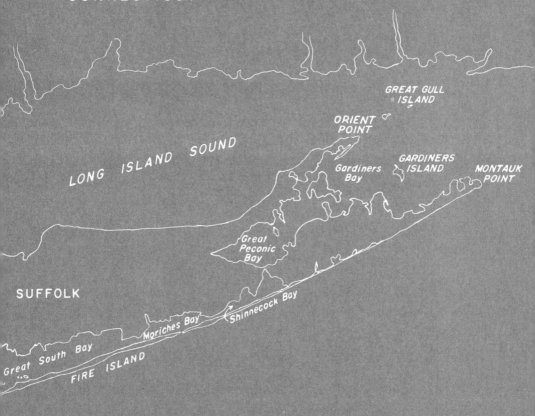

CONNECTICUT

GREAT GULL
ISLAND

ORIENT
POINT

LONG ISLAND SOUND

GARDINERS
ISLAND

MONTAUK
POINT

Gardiners
Bay

Great
Peconic
Bay

SUFFOLK

Shinnecock Bay

Moriches Bay

Great South Bay

FIRE ISLAND

ATLANTIC OCEAN

Enjoying Birds

AROUND NEW YORK CITY

Companion to this volume

ENJOYING BIRDS IN UPSTATE NEW YORK

by
Olin Sewall Pettingill, Jr., and Sally F. Hoyt
published by the Laboratory of Ornithology, Cornell University,
33 Sapsucker Woods Road, Ithaca, New York 14850

Enjoying Birds

AROUND NEW YORK CITY

AN AID TO RECOGNIZING, WATCHING, FINDING,

AND ATTRACTING BIRDS IN NEW YORK CITY, LONG ISLAND,

THE UPSTATE COUNTIES OF WESTCHESTER, PUTNAM,

DUTCHESS, ROCKLAND, AND ORANGE, AND NEARBY

POINTS IN NEW JERSEY AND CONNECTICUT

BY

Robert S. Arbib, Jr., Olin Sewall Pettingill, Jr.,

and Sally Hoyt Spofford for the Laboratory

of Ornithology, Cornell University

Ithaca, New York

ILLUSTRATED

HOUGHTON MIFFLIN COMPANY BOSTON
THE RIVERSIDE PRESS CAMBRIDGE
1966

CONTENTS

Illustrations by William C. Dilger
unless otherwise specified

LIST OF MAPS

Enjoying Birds

AROUND NEW YORK CITY

BARN OWL

HOW TO RECOGNIZE AND WATCH BIRDS

THE BEGINNING BIRD WATCHER may feel overwhelmed when told that there are about 400 different kinds, or *species,* of birds for him to recognize around New York City. But he should take heart! Neither he nor anyone else can see all of them at once.

As we shall point out presently, there are certain elementary facts about the distribution of birds in season and place that make it rather unusual for anyone to see many more than 100 on a given day in a given area. Furthermore, the species are not at all as confusing as they might seem. There are species called woodpeckers which have much in common by way of form and behavior, just as there are several species called wrens, several species called vireos, and so on. In New York City and vicinity these groups of similar, closely related species, or *families,* total 57 — by no means an overwhelming number. As soon as the beginning bird watcher has identified, say, a woodpecker, he knows the general appearance of all 9 woodpeckers found in this area, and is well on his way to finding what the particular species is. Once he has determined it, the identification of the other 8 woodpeckers becomes easier because he already has a basis for comparison. It will be the same way with his identification of expected wrens (5 species) and vireos (6 species).

Assuming that you, the reader, are a beginner in bird watching — a hobby in which literally millions find recreation — we are providing herewith some instructions and advice on how you may go about identifying and watching birds. Later in this book we shall tell you about some familiar birds of the New York City area, where to find birds, when to expect certain birds during the calendar year, and how to attract birds. Reading this book may be your homework — your preparation for enjoying birds around New York City.

KNOW THE SEASONAL CATEGORIES

In any given locality bird life falls into seasonal categories. There are, first of all, *permanent residents,* which are found at all seasons of the year. In our New York City region these include the Black Duck, Sparrow Hawk, Herring Gull, Hairy and Downy Woodpeckers, Blue Jay, Common Crow, Black-capped Chickadee, Tufted Titmouse, White-breasted Nuthatch, Starling, House Sparrow, Cardinal, Song Sparrow, and a number of other species. In the case of a few species, such as the Blue Jay, some individuals may be permanent residents in the area, while other individuals of the same species may move on. Other species such as the Herring Gull, although seen the year round, may actually be in large part two separate populations that replace each other seasonally.

Summer residents are birds that return each summer to nest after having wintered farther south. Among the more familiar species in this category are the Chimney Swift, Barn Swallow, Catbird, Wood Thrush, Yellow Warbler, Baltimore Oriole, and Chipping Sparrow.

In spring and fall we see *migrants* or *transients* — birds passing through between their southern wintering grounds and breeding areas farther north. Many shorebirds and warblers are in this category, as are the White-crowned and Fox Sparrows. Certain transients are absent or far less common either in the spring or fall, depending on their migration routes and other factors.

In the summer or winter we look for visitors or *visitants*. Late summer visitants may include northward-wandering, immature herons, eagles, and a few seabirds. Or they may include hurricane-carried strays — for example, Gull-billed Terns and Sooty Terns — from southern coastal waters. In winter we look for such visitants from the north as loons, grebes, many diving ducks, and the Rough-legged Hawk, Purple Sandpiper, Northern Shrike, Tree Sparrow, Lapland Longspur, and Snow Bunting. In winter too we may expect from the north what we call invasions or *incursions* by the Snowy Owl and various finches — the Evening and Pine Grosbeaks, Common Redpoll, Pine Siskin, and the Red and White-winged Crossbills, to name a few. Of course, small numbers of these species usually appear almost every winter, but it is only at irregular intervals, sometimes with many years intervening, that we observe widespread incursions.

Lastly, there are birds categorized as *accidentals*. An accidental is a bird appearing far outside its normal range. Examples of recent accidental records in the New York City area are the Yellow-nosed Albatross observed

NORTHERN SHRIKE

off Jones Beach on May 29, 1960, the Lewis' Woodpecker observed at Ossining in the autumn of 1954, and the Sage Thrasher netted and banded at Tiana Beach on Long Island in October 1958. (Quite often birds reported as accidentals may actually be fugitives from private cages or public zoos. Every bird watcher in the New York City area sooner or later experiences the momentary shock of encountering the odd Brazilian Cardinal, Java Sparrow, or Budgerigar in the foliage! But we do not call any such fugitive an accidental.) Aware of the possibility that he may see an accidental, the beginning watcher is apt to turn a common species into an accidental for the simple reason that the species is in a plumage that he does not recognize. Probably every bird watcher has made this mistake in his learning period. However, birds can fly, can go practically anywhere; therefore it is just as possible for the keen-eyed beginner to see a bona fide rarity as the veteran bird watcher.

You should learn what birds to expect during the season in a given locality. The Calendar Graph in this book (p. 131) or seasonal lists put out by bird clubs and museums will be helpful. Absolutely essential is the book *Birds of the New York Area* by John Bull with its detailed discussion of the current status of each species on the local list. (See "Sources of Information on Birds" at the back of this book for the date and publisher of the work and all other books to be mentioned later in the text.) An additional help to you will be a visit to the American Museum of Natural History, where you can study a display of mounted specimens of almost all the species in the New York area. The display will help you particularly in learning the actual sizes of different birds.

KNOW SOME OF THE HABITAT PREFERENCES

No bird is found everywhere, in every type of environment. While it is true that certain species during migration will appear in unexpected places, on the whole most species are quite selective, preferring one habitat to another. The wren you see in a marsh is almost certain to be different from the one in a dooryard, or the one in a deep coniferous forest. The hawk you watch soaring high over open fields will not be the same as the hawk you glimpse dashing through thick woods. Some of the elementary ornithology texts, such as Arthur A. Allen's *The Book of Bird Life,* will tell you which species prefer coniferous or deciduous woods, open fields, marshes, shorelines, and other places.

CLASSIFY BIRDS INTO FAMILIES

Classifying birds into families is a useful procedure. For one thing it points out characteristics that are significant in narrowing down a bird to a choice among a small number of species; and, for another, it helps to explain why all black-colored birds are not blackbirds, why herons are not cranes, why night-hawks are not hawks. A simple and inexpensive guide to assist you with recognition of families is Roger Tory Peterson's *How to Know the Birds*.

Families are determined by obvious characteristics, particularly of form and behavior. The shape of the bill will often be a characteristic. Sharp, chisel-shaped bills for drilling holes and securing insect larvae in bark and wood mark the family of woodpeckers; slender, pin-pointed bills for seizing insects, the family of warblers; stout, conical bills for crushing seeds, the family of finches and sparrows.

Knowing what the bird does will also help you determine the family. Woodpeckers jerk their way up tree trunks, using their tails as props; they may move down, but never headfirst. Nuthatches move smoothly and rapidly on tree trunks and limbs in any direction — up, down, and around — without using their tails; they may even go down a tree headfirst. Vireos resemble warblers but their behavior is more deliberate or unhurried.

IDENTIFY THE SPECIES

Once you have placed the bird in its proper family, you must determine certain peculiarities that will narrow it down to a species.

Size. Estimate the size, not by guessing it in inches, but by comparing it to that of a common bird such as a House Sparrow, Common Crow, or a goose.

Shape. Observe the shape. Is the bird chunky or slender? Its tail long or short, and the end round, square, or notched? Its legs long or short?

Color and Color Pattern. If the bird is in the gull family, you need to note the color of its bill and legs and its wing-tip pattern. If the bird is in the vireo family, you must see whether or not it has wing bars, eye-ring, eye stripe, and a yellowish wash below. In each family you look for special features of color and color pattern that distinguish its species. Those you look for in the gull family differ from those in the vireo family.

Song and Other Vocalizations. The song and other vocal sounds of the birds are important because they are never the same in two species. Some of the smaller flycatchers are so much alike in appearance that they are more readily recognized by their sounds. Moreover, birds are often obscured by foliage or far from view in a wood. By hearing them you can frequently make accurate identifications.

Locomotion. A considerable number of species have peculiarities of flight. The Eastern Kingbird flies with rapidly quivering wings, as does the Eastern Meadowlark. In the warbler family the Ovenbird and water-thrushes walk and the Yellow and Myrtle Warblers hop.

Behavior. The way a bird behaves may give a good clue to identification. The Palm Warbler is one of the few members of its family to wag its tail. Among the tree-climbing birds, the Brown Creeper almost invariably starts near the base of the trunk; when through climbing that tree, it flies *down* to the base of the next one to begin again.

Habitat. Where a bird is found should be taken into account, for it may well be another clue to its identity.

Quite obviously you cannot set out to identify birds without some assistance. This brings us to the next topic.

TUFTED
TITMOUSE

AIDS FOR IDENTIFICATION

Field Guides. Absolutely essential is a good field guide in which all the regularly expected species are pictured and their distinguishing characteristics pointed out. Strongly recommended is Roger Tory Peterson's *A Field Guide to the Birds* — a compact volume with color plates comparing similar species and a highly condensed text packed with information on appearance, song, habitat, range, etc. Complementing this book with additional pictures in color and useful information on voice, habits, nests, and general ecology, are the two Audubon Bird Guides (Water Birds, Land Birds) by Richard H. Pough. If one wishes to be completely equipped to identify possible accidentals, he might later add two other Peterson volumes, *A Field Guide to Western Birds* and *A Field Guide to the Birds of Britain and Europe,* which also include many local species.

Birds Song Records. Now available is an album, *A Field Guide to Bird Songs,* containing two 12-inch LP records of the songs and calls of most of our local species. The records are arranged to accompany Peterson's *Field Guide* page by page. Another record, *Bird Songs in Your Garden,* has the songs of some of the commonest birds. One side gives the songs identified by the human voice; the other side plays the same songs unidentified so that you may learn to identify them yourself. The beginning bird watcher, by playing these records repeatedly, will be able to remember the songs and calls when he hears them in the field. Next to listening to the bird itself sing over and over again, there is no better way of learning its song.

Binoculars. A necessity for successful bird identification is a binocular. For ordinary purposes the 7 × 35 with central focusing is recommended. The "7×" means that the binocular has a magnifying power of 7 times, thus making a bird 70 feet away seem as close as 10; the figure "35" signifies the diameter of the objective and indicates a brightness value of 25 — determined by dividing the diameter of the objective by the magnifying power (7) and squaring the quotient (5). The greater the brightness in a binocular, the more desirable it is. The lenses should be coated to ensure greater brightness and reduce glare. Central focusing enables the user to keep a bird in focus as it moves rapidly.

For following birds fairly close at hand in woods or thickets, the 6 × 30 binocular is usually better since it provides wider field and less magnification. On the other hand, for identifying birds far out on a lake, the 8 × 30, 8 × 40, and 10 × 50 are better because of their greater magnification; the 10× must be held very steady, since its field is not increased in proportion to its magnification.

If you expect to be looking for birds at great distances, you should consider getting a telescope such as the so-called "spotting scope," 16 mm. model, with interchangeable eyepieces having magnifications of 13×, 20×, 27×, and 35×. A tripod support is necessary.

SOME MISCELLANEOUS SUGGESTIONS

Look for Birds in the Early Morning. The first two hours after daybreak are the best, especially in the late spring and early summer. Birds are more active and singing is at its height. There is usually less wind to interfere with your hearing; the foliage is consequently quieter, and you can see birds in trees.

Bring Birds into View by "Squeaking." Frequently small birds whose habitats are thick woods, thickets, or tall grass may be momentarily brought into view by your making squeaking sounds, such as by kissing noisily the back of your hand, or by whispering loudly and repeatedly a sound that resembles *spish.* Sounds of this sort tend to startle or alarm a bird, perhaps arouse its curiosity and cause it to investigate the source.

Use the Car as a Blind. A bird is much less disturbed by a car than by a person. When a bird you want to watch closely comes into view from your car, you should stay in it, moving the car as near to the bird as you can.

Keep a Checklist and Take Notes. Have with you on each trip a checklist of the birds of your region. (A supply of checklists for the New York City area may be obtained from the Linnaean Society of New York, American Museum of Natural History.) Mark on the list the date of the trip, hours involved, and weather conditions. Check off the species as you see them. Also take with you a pocket notebook, using a page for each species. Put down any observations that seem at variance with your field guide. If you have difficulty remembering songs, write them down *as they sound to you.* On successive trips add further information on the same pages. The checklists and notebook at the end of the season will stand as a personal record of your field trips and a useful basis on which to begin the corresponding season the next year.

NORTHERN
WATERTHRUSH

THE CHALLENGE IN BIRD IDENTIFICATION

Any bird watcher, even one who is "advanced," has difficulty recognizing all the birds he sees. This is partly because certain species have immature or winter plumages quite different from the more familiar and commonly pictured breeding plumages, partly because birds are relatively silent except at the start of the nesting season, and partly because birds may make themselves evident only in unfavorable light or at great distances.

Young birds of many species recently out of the nest wear plumages that are heavily streaked or mottled, or have dull hues scarcely suggesting the bright colors of their parents. While in these plumages young birds of several species can look very much alike and sometimes be practically indistinguishable. Many warblers forsake their conspicuous garb of the breeding season for plumages washed with blending, nondescript shades of yellow, green, gray, and brown.

All birds have vocalization other than song. We usually designate them as "calls" for want of a better term, and we are likely to hear these calls in any season. To the beginner they may sound like so many squawks, whistles, chirps, and so on, but to the experienced bird watcher they have qualities of pitch or tone, accent, and duration that are peculiar to each species.

A bird in silhouette on the horizon or standing on the shore against the sunlight may seem impossible to identify, yet more often than not it will have something about it — the way it moves its wings or holds its head, its stance or its length of bill in proportion to head — that will reveal its identity.

The fact that there is a marked degree of difficulty in recognizing different birds makes bird identification a personal challenge — just as any sport or hobby that requires training, experience, and skill is a challenge. It is a challenge to your observational powers to distinguish one fall warbler from another, to detect the *pink* call of a migrating Bobolink as it passes overhead out of view, to recognize the silhouette of a Belted Kingfisher flying against the sunset. If there were no challenge to bird identification, bird watching would be dull indeed.

SOME FAMILIAR BIRDS AROUND NEW YORK CITY

Illustrations by Orville O. Rice

COMMON LOON, *Gavia immer*

Goose size, but rides lower in the water. Commonly found in bays, rivers, harbors, and offshore waters in migration and in winter (sometimes abundant, particularly in eastern Long Island). Occasionally summers. Less frequent in freshwater, but may visit any reservoir or lake. During migration moves in considerable numbers over ocean and Long Island Sound shores, in far lesser numbers along the Hudson River valley. Often seen on early mornings in the spring high overhead, flying in ones and twos northward to breeding grounds.

In spring and summer, adults (both sexes) have black heads and necks, checkered black and white backs, and white underparts. Immatures and adults in fall and winter are gray above with white underparts. The stout, pointed bill and short neck are characteristic. (The Red-throated Loon, *G. stellata,* a winter visitant, frequents saltwater exclusively, is a smaller, less robust bird, paler above, with a more slender, uptilted bill.) Loons rarely call in our area, except overhead in spring, when they give their high-pitched, quavering laugh, or yodel.

Rarely seen on land except when nesting, but they are skillful swimmers, swift, strong fliers, and efficient divers. Loons can stay under water up to 3 minutes and reach depths of 200 feet in this manner.

Food in this area consists mainly of fish, shrimps, and crabs.

HORNED GREBE, *Podiceps auritus*

Size of a small duck (teal) but with a slender neck. The commonest of three local grebes. Found from September through May (most numerous in November and April) almost anywhere from patches of open water in frozen reservoirs to breaking surf along the shore. Most frequent in salt-water — bays, harbors, and the ocean. Being rather tame, it can often be observed singly or in small flocks about piers, pilings, and jetties. When with other water birds, as is often the case, it is the smallest species.

Sexes alike. Winter birds, such as we usually see, have top of head, hind neck, and back gray; rest of plumage white. Neck slender; bill pointed and shorter than head. Summer birds, rarely seen here, have upperparts glossy black, with wide, black cheek ruffs and large tawny patches above eyes curving upward into "horns"; throat, breast, and sides chestnut; underparts white. During flight, which is weak and fluttery, winter or summer birds reveal large white wing patches. Normally silent.

The similarly small Pied-billed Grebe, *Podilymbus podiceps,* is a grayish-brown plumper bird, in summer with a black chin and a black band around its short blunt "chicken" bill. It prefers freshwater and occasionally breeds in our weedy ponds and marshes. Rare in winter.

The Horned Grebe feeds under water, mainly on fish and small marine life, diving with a little preliminary jump to depths usually under 25 feet.

GREAT BLUE HERON, *Ardea herodias*

Erroneously called Crane. The largest of our local wading birds, standing about 4 feet tall, with wingspread of 6 feet. Occurs throughout the area, frequenting marshy waterways, pond and lakeshores, salt meadows and creeks, and bay flats, wherever shallow waters permit feeding. A common migrant, most abundant in April and September; present throughout the summer but breeding very locally; also present in small numbers in winter, although rare after December. A good one-day count in September might total 50 to 60 individuals.

Sexes alike. Readily identified by the great size, over-all blue and gray coloration, long legs and neck, and long pointed bill. Both immatures and adults show white on the head and neck, but only adults have white on the top of the head. During flight, which is slow and majestic on noticeably broad wings, the neck is drawn up and the legs extend well beyond the tail. Usually silent.

The Great Blue Heron searches for much of its food, which consists of animal life, while wading in shallow water, sometimes up to its chest. It frequently remains motionless for long periods awaiting its prey, which is captured with a sudden, swordlike thrust of the powerful beak. Fish, frogs, tadpoles, and various other small animals are taken extensively. Often the bird forsakes water to feed on land. Then it consumes mice, shrews, snakes, and insects.

GREEN HERON, *Butorides virescens*

A small, short-legged heron, about 17 inches long with neck extended, but usually stands with neck drawn in, appearing shorter and hunched. Our most widespread heron, summer resident throughout the area, frequenting the shores of streams, ponds, and marshes both salt and fresh.

Adults and immatures of both sexes are dark-colored at a distance, but close up show white stripe down throat and breast, reddish neck, yellow legs (orange-red in breeding males). Back and wings of adults slaty green (wings of immatures speckled). Habit of twitching tail when alarmed is distinctive. As with other herons, flight is steady, with head pulled back to shoulders, legs extended beyond tail, and wings bent down toward tips; at a distance remarkably crowlike. Principal call is a harsh *skeeow*, often heard after dark.

Nests occasionally in colonies but more often in solitary pairs in a thickly foliaged bush or tree, 3 to 30 feet above ground. Nest is loosely made, shallow platform of sticks. Eggs: 3 to 5, pale greenish blue. Incubation: about 20 days, probably by both sexes. Both parents feed the young, which leave the nest after 15 or 16 days, before they can fly.

Small fish compose most of its food, but many crayfish and insects, both aquatic and terrestrial, are also taken. The Green Heron fishes by waiting motionless until its prey swims within striking range, then captures it with a lightning thrust of its bill.

BLACK-CROWNED NIGHT HERON,
Nycticorax nycticorax

A medium-sized, short-legged, chunky heron, about 2 feet in length, with a stout bill. Frequents almost any habitat, fresh or salt, where it can wade to feed. A common summer resident throughout our area. Some individuals regularly winter, usually roosting in tall evergreens.

Adults (sexes alike) have head and crest dark glossy green, with inconspicuous white plumes, forehead and stripe through eye white; upperparts greenish black, underparts white or creamy gray; wings, lower back, and tail bluish gray; bill black and legs yellow. Immature birds are noticeably streaked dusky brownish and buff, with bill olive and legs buffy gray. Voice is a sharp *quock* often heard at dusk or after dark. The somewhat similar but much less common Yellow-crowned Night Heron, *Nyctanassa violacea*, has an over-all dark gray appearance with face black and yellowish crest and cheek patches, shorter bill, and longer legs that project beyond tail in flight. Young streaked.

The Black-crown nests in colonies of a few to over 100 pairs, often with other herons. The nests, which may be anywhere from ground to high in trees, are platforms of twigs lined with grasses. Eggs: 3 to 5, pale blue-green, laid mainly in late April. Incubation: 24 to 26 days, by both sexes. Both parents feed the young, which fly in about 6 weeks.

The food consists mainly of fish, frogs, mollusks, crustaceans, and insects.

MUTE SWAN, *Cygnus olor*

Our largest all-white bird, nearly 5 feet in length. Originally introduced from Europe for esthetic purposes, it is now naturalized and a common permanent resident on our park and estate ponds, lakes, and tidal estuaries. In winter it gathers on open water of our harbors and bays, being most numerous in southern Suffolk County.

Adults of both sexes have an orange bill with a black knob and black legs. Immatures have a black bill and dirty-gray plumage. When taking flight, Mute Swans require a long run, during which they slap the water noisily with their wing tips. They are normally silent, but have a loud warning snort or hiss.

In spring the wintering flocks break up and pairs proceed to their nesting grounds, selecting undisturbed margins of ponds and marshy islands. The nest is a bulky mound of plant debris constructed by both sexes. Eggs: 5 to 11, pale gray or faintly blue-green. Incubation: about 35 days, by female. Both parents care for the fluffy grayish cygnets, which take to the water soon after hatching and fly in 4½ months. The parents are very aggressive during the nesting season and may attack intruders, including human beings.

The food consists mostly of plant life growing in shallow water.

The smaller Whistling Swan, *Cygnus columbianus,* is a rare migrant, usually seen on coastal ponds. Also white, it has a black bill with yellow spots and holds its head at a sharper angle to its slimmer, less curved neck. The immature, often mistaken for the immature Mute, can be distinguished by the way it holds its head.

CANADA GOOSE, *Branta canadensis*

Large waterfowl, about 3 feet long. Abundant spring and fall migrant in the New York area, where V-shaped flocks may be seen passing overhead between their breeding grounds in Canada and wintering areas in southern United States. Large flocks congregate annually in rye fields around Mecox Bay in Suffolk County in late winter and early spring. Small flocks winter in sheltered bays.

Adults and immatures of both sexes are brownish gray with black necks and heads with conspicuous white cheek patches. Flight call is a clear, ringing *ker-honk.* The similar but smaller Brant, *B. bernicla,* has a shorter neck, an inconspicuous neck spot, and black breast. It flies in loose flocks and gathers in wintering congregations of up to 25,000 along the south shore of Long Island. Call is a musical chortle.

No truly wild Canada Geese breed in the area, but semi-domesticated, free-flying birds nest in scattered local ponds and marshes. Nests are near water, usually on grassy tussocks. Eggs: usually 5 to 8, from greenish yellow to creamy buff. Incubation: 30 to 36 days, by female. During incubation the gander remains on guard nearby. Both parents assist in caring for the young.

Geese sometimes eat insects and snails, but much of their food consists of seeds, grasses, and plant roots obtained in shallow water or grain taken in upland fields.

MALLARD, *Anas platyrhynchos*

A large duck, about 23 inches long, often semidomesticated. Our common "park" duck, breeding regularly in fresh and brackish marshes and the vicinity of ponds. Occurs more commonly in migration. Remains throughout the winter in fair numbers wherever there is open water.

Male has a glossy-green head and neck, white collar, gray wings with a white-bordered violet-blue speculum, whitish tail, dark red breast, yellow bill, and orange feet. Female and immatures streaked brown all over, but with same white-bordered speculum and white tail, helpful for identification in flight. Call of the female is a loud, sharp *quack;* of the male, a quieter, mellowed *queeb.* When alarmed, Mallards spring into flight from the water, without a takeoff run.

Nest is on dry ground, frequently but not always near water, in a depression usually well concealed in grasses or bushes; made of grass stems, leaves, and other plant materials, and lined with down. Eggs: 6 to 15 (averaging 10), pale greenish buff. Incubation: 27 to 28 days, by female. Only one brood a year is raised, which is the rule among waterfowl. The young fly in about 2 months.

Mallards, like other "puddle ducks," feed from the water's surface by tipping up. Food consists primarily of seeds, but leaves and stems of aquatic plants are often consumed.

BLACK DUCK, *Anas rubripes*

Same size as the Mallard. Our most abundant breeding waterfowl, nesting mainly in salt marshes, and one of the most widespread the year round, the local population being augmented in spring and fall by migrant flocks. In winter, common on lakes, reservoirs, tidal creeks, bays, and often in large rafts with other waterfowl offshore in the ocean and Long Island Sound.

Sexes alike. A swift-flying, wary duck, appearing black in distance but actually dark brown all over and finely streaked, with a purplish, black-bordered speculum, yellow bill, and yellow feet (red in breeding male). The silvery underwing linings help to identify it in flight. Voice like the Mallard's.

Nest, usually well concealed in an isolated spot on high

ground adjacent to a marsh or stream, is a bulky saucer of dead vegetation, lined with down. Eggs: usually 8 to 10, cream to greenish buff. Incubation: 26 to 28 days, by female. After hatching the ducklings are led by female to the nearest water, where they generally remain and are cared for by her until able to fly.

Black ducks feed extensively on aquatic plants such as wild celery, pondweed, and eelgrass, but in winter take shellfish and other animal life from the tidal flats.

AMERICAN WIDGEON, *Mareca americana*

Also called Baldpate. Slightly smaller than a Mallard. Locally abundant in fall and spring, wintering in some numbers on sheltered waters. In fall, flocks up to 500 or more frequent lakes, reservoirs, and bays, favoring especially such places as Playland Lake, Jamaica Bay Wildlife Refuge, Hempstead Reservoir, Tobay Pond, Carman's River, and Mill Neck. Breeds in upland fields only at Jamaica Bay Wildlife Refuge.

Adult male pinkish brown, with gray head, white crown, glossy green cheek patch, and black tail area. When bird is at rest or in flight, a broad white area on the inner wing is visible. Female paler, lacking white crown and green cheek patch. Immatures lack white wing area and have a whitish belly. Widgeons fly in tight, swift formations. Call, a whistled *wheu, wheu, wheu.* The somewhat similar European Widgeon, *M. penelope,* is a rare visitor from the Old World. The male is distinctively gray, with rufous head, buffy crown, and pink breast. The female differs slightly from our American species in having a reddish cast on head.

Nest of the American Widgeon is a hollow on dry ground near water, lined with grass and down. Eggs: usually 9 to 11, creamy white. Incubation: about 25 days, by female. The young are cared for by the female and attain flight in about 7 weeks.

Eelgrass, wild celery, and pondweed are favorite foods, obtained by tipping up in shallow water. Grains and tender grasses are also sought by foraging in upland fields.

GREATER SCAUP, *Aythya marila*

Also called Bluebill or Broadbill. Smaller than a Mallard and chunkier. Essentially a saltwater species in our area, and by far our most abundant migrant waterfowl. Present from early fall through midspring in our bays, rivers, harbors, and in lesser numbers on freshwater. Concentrations of 50,000 or more winter in western Long Island Sound, other thousands frequent Long Island's south shore bays. A few summer, as nonbreeders.

Male is distinguished by iridescent black head, neck, and breast, pale blue bill, gray back, white sides and belly, and black tail. Female generally brown above with noticeable white above base of bill. In flight, both sexes show a broad white wing stripe. Usually seen on water in densely packed flocks, often 1000 birds per acre. Flight is swift and erratic, in tight, veering flocks, with loud rustling sounds. While migrating, normally at great height, they move steadily in large masses, often with a broad front. Scaups are usually silent, especially by day, but when alarmed give a harsh *scaup*. The males utter low-toned purring and whistling notes during courtship.

The very similar Lesser Scaup, *A. affinis,* has a head with steeper forehead, purple reflection on head (green in Greater), and a shorter wing stripe. It is less common than the Greater and frequents freshwater more often.

Scaups are expert divers, like other saltwater ducks, capable of descending to depths of 20 feet and remaining submerged 30 seconds or more. They are omnivorous, taking such food items as wild celery, sedges, clams, snails, crustaceans, and insects.

WHITE-WINGED SCOTER, *Melanitta deglandi*

Almost the size of a Mallard but heavier in appearance. The most abundant of three similar species of large predominantly black sea ducks, sometimes called sea coots, that frequent our offshore waters from October through April, commonly riding the swells beyond the breaker lines. White-winged Scoters often make up most of the scoter flocks — with individuals numbering in the tens of thousands — that winter occasionally around Montauk Point. They are present in smaller numbers in sheltered saltwater and are rare in freshwater.

Male, all-black, with large white wing patches, a small white eye spot, and knobbed bill. Female, dark brown, with wing patches and two pale face spots. Immatures similar to females but have whiter face spots. The male Surf Scoter, *M. perspicillata,* is all-black with white forehead and crown patches; the female resembles the female White-winged Scoter, but lacks the wing patches. The male Common Scoter, *Oidemia nigra,* is all-black (and our only duck so colored); the female is dusky brown. Scoters have a variety of calls ranging from melodious whistles to croaks.

All three scoters occur in mixed flocks, the Common Scoter, despite its name, being the least numerous. All scoters fly swiftly in loose flocks or strings, low over the water.

Large flocks of scoters often move from one feeding ground to another by breaking up and shuttling in smaller groups. Their food consists primarily of mollusks — such as mussels, clams, and scallops, and many kinds of crabs, which are obtained by diving deeply, sometimes to 20 feet.

RED-BREASTED MERGANSER, *Mergus serrator*

Also called Sheldrake. About the size of a Mallard but much slimmer. The commonest of our three mergansers, and one of our most abundant sea ducks. Widespread in the fall, winter, and spring on the ocean and sound and in bays and harbors, gathering by many thousands, particularly offshore in eastern Suffolk County. Less common on freshwater.

A longish, slender-bodied duck with a crested head and slim pink bill. The male has a glossy-green head, white collar, and deep reddish breast; the female and immatures are grayish with reddish-brown head and neck, the neck color blending into the white throat and breast. When flying, the Red-breasted, like the other two mergansers, shows white wing patches and takes a direct course with head and neck extended in a straight line. Though usually silent, its most common call is a hoarse croak.

The Common Merganser, *M. merganser,* is predominantly a freshwater visitant. The male has a black head (no crest) tinged with green. Upperparts are generally black, breast and belly white. The female and immatures are gray and white, with reddish-brown crested heads contrasting sharply with white breasts.

Fish make up much of the food of the Red-breasted Merganser, although mollusks, crustaceans, and some aquatic insects are taken. When raiding a school of fish, a whole flock of mergansers may be seen following along excitedly on the surface, the birds in the rear flying forward to land and dive ahead of those in front.

SHARP-SHINNED HAWK, *Accipiter striatus*

Slightly larger than a Robin but slimmer, with broad rounded wings and a long tail *square*-tipped when closed. No longer common but present the year round wherever woodlands remain, even in urban parks and cemeteries. In greatest numbers during migrations, especially in the fall when passing along ridges. Uncommon in the summer and rare in winter.

Sexes identical in color but female larger. Adults bluish black above, barred with brown below. Immatures brown above, heavily streaked with brown below. Like all accipiters, the Sharp-shin flies with a series of rapid wingbeats, alternating with short glides. Occasionally it soars in tight circles on extended fixed wings. It is also remarkably agile in streaking through dense woodlands at high speed. The only confusing species is the Cooper's Hawk, *A. cooperii,* the male of which may be the same size as the female Sharp-shin. The main distinction between the species is in the tail when closed — *rounded* at the tip in the Cooper's. The voice of the Sharp-shin is a piercing *cac, cac, cac.*

Nest is in a tree, often a conifer, usually 30 to 60 feet from the ground in a dense woodland adjacent to a clearing; a shallow platform of twigs, lined with little if any fine plant materials. Eggs: 3 to 6, bluish white to cream, splotched with brown. Incubation: 21 to 24 days, by both sexes. The young leave the nest in about 4 weeks.

Food consists of small mammals, large insects, and small birds. Occasionally a Sharp-shinned Hawk will decimate winter birds frequenting a suburban feeder.

RED-TAILED HAWK, *Buteo jamaicensis*

Larger than a Common Crow. Occurs chiefly as a migrant in spring and fall, when it may be seen soaring high overhead on thermal currents or following updrafts along ridges. A regular but uncommon winter resident. Frequents less disturbed woodlands and woodland edges where scattered pairs still nest, more open country — including marshlands — in winter.

This is the largest of the heavy-winged, short-tailed hawks that frequently soar in flight. Tail of adults is chestnut-red above and pale, unbarred beneath; tail of immatures is strongly barred. Both adults and immatures have a prominent streaked band across center of light belly. Confusing species are Broad-winged and Red-shouldered Hawks, *B. platypterus* and *B. lineatus.* Former is much smaller and has *wide* bands of black and white on tail; latter has many *narrow* tail bands, also reddish shoulder patches and underparts. Immatures of both species evenly streaked below. Voice of the Red-tail is a high-pitched, squealing whistle.

Nest, built of sticks, twigs, and grasses, is usually at considerable height, sometimes 60 to 70 feet, in a large tree. Eggs: 2 to 4, dull white, irregularly spotted with brown. Incubation: 28 to 32 days, by both sexes.

Small mammals, such as mice and red squirrels, and insects make up much of its food. Often snakes and frogs are eaten, and occasionally a small bird. This is a very beneficial hawk; mice are its favorite food.

MARSH HAWK, *Circus cyaneus*

The length of a Common Crow but slenderer, with long wings and long tail. Seen most often quartering low over open country, showing a distinctive white rump, but sometimes observed resting on a fence post or some similarly low perch. Although gradually decreasing in numbers, still a

widespread summer resident in coastal marshes, a common migrant over the outer beaches in the fall, and an uncommon winter resident. More numerous on Long Island than elsewhere.

Adult male gray above, lighter below, with rusty streaks. Female and immatures brown above (the color deeper and richer in immatures), buffy below, with brown streaks and bars. Marsh Hawks have a facial disk that gives them an owlish look. They fly with a slow, butterfly-like grace, their wings elevated slightly above the horizontal in a shallow V. In the distance the lighter-colored males with their black-tipped wings suggest gulls. The most commonly heard call is a high staccato shriek, *kee-kee-kee-kee.*

Nest is on the ground in a marsh or field near water and concealed by tall grassy or shrubby growth. An accumulation of sticks, weeds, and grasses, cupped slightly enough to serve as an egg receptacle. Eggs: usually 5, bluish white, rarely marked with brown. Incubation: 29 to 30 days, by female. The young are fed by both parents and fly in 7 or 8 weeks.

Food consists mainly of rodents, but includes reptiles, frogs, grasshoppers, and some small birds.

SPARROW HAWK, *Falco sparverius*

About the size of a Robin, but with longer, pointed wings and tail. The most widespread hawk, present the year round but more common in migration, occurring almost anywhere, even in urban parks; prefers open fields, woodland edges, meadowlands, and (especially in fall) the outer beaches. It shows little fear of man and is frequently seen perched on a telephone pole or wire beside a heavily traveled highway.

A very colorful bird. The male has a reddish-brown back and tail, blue-gray wings, and spotted breast and belly. The female and immatures have the entire back, tail, and inner half of wings reddish brown finely barred with black. Underparts with brown streaks. Head of both sexes streaked or blotched with chestnut, gray, black, and white. This is the only small hawk having a red tail. A variety of call notes is given, the most familiar being a high-pitched *killy, killy, killy, killy.*

Nest is generally in a natural cavity in a tree or an abandoned woodpecker hole, occasionally in a birdhouse, 10 to 40 feet from the ground. Eggs: 4 to 7, white to reddish white, heavily blotched with brown and lavender. Incubation: about 29 days, by both sexes.

This highly beneficial hawk (it is actually a falcon) feeds extensively on insects. Other food, taken in lesser amounts, includes mice, snakes, and frogs. As it searches for prey over a field, it often hovers in midair while studying the ground intently.

RING-NECKED PHEASANT, *Phasianus colchicus*

An introduced species of mixed Asiatic lineage, now a completely naturalized and common permanent resident, except in wholly urban areas. Our only truly wild pheasant, it prefers open brushy country, but is equally at home in parks, on golf courses, and even in bayberry cover along the outer beaches.

Unmistakable chicken-like birds with small heads and long tapering tails. Male (35 inches in length, including conspicuously long tail) has rich colors above and below ranging from metallic copper to varying shades of red, yellow, and blue, and numberless spots and bars; head glossy dark green with large red wattles; neck with white collar. Female (22 inches) and immatures are brown, paler below, and variously spotted and streaked. Pheasants, when disturbed, take flight with a clatter of wings and proceed swiftly out of sight, never rising far above the ground. The usual call is a ringing *cuk-cuk*.

Each male pheasant is usually mated to several females. Nest is a grass-lined hollow on the ground, concealed under shrubs or tall grass. Eggs: usually 10 or 11, olive-brown to pale blue. Incubation: 23 to 25 days, by female. The chicks follow the female and forage for food soon after hatching.

Pheasants feed like domestic fowl, picking up seeds, grain, buds, plant shoots, small fruits, and insects as they walk over fields, along parkway borders, often in full view, especially in mornings and evenings.

CLAPPER RAIL, *Rallus longirostris*

About 17 inches long. The commonest rail, summer resident in salt and brackish marshes but most abundant in the marshes along the western south shore of Long Island. Recorded each winter in small numbers.

Sexes alike. Face gray and back grayish brown, breast pinkish brown, flanks barred gray and white, undertail coverts conspicuously white. Bill long, yellowish, decurved at tip. The legs are long and the feet large. The slightly larger King Rail, *R. elegans,* frequents freshwater marshes but is much rarer. In general it is more richly brown with a brighter, more reddish breast and a chestnut coloring on the wings. Both rails are heard more often than seen. The Clapper's strident, percussive *cac-cac-cac-cac,* decreasing in speed and volume, can be heard across the tidal marshes at any time but most often at dusk and frequently at night. Careful search for the source of the call will often reveal the stealthy bird picking its jerky way, with tail high, along a marshy creek or mud bank.

Nest is a high, rounded platform of dead vegetation in a marsh concealed under an arch of reeds. Eggs: 9 to 12, buffy

with brown spots. Incubation: 21 to 23 days, by both parents. The chicks leave the nest soon after hatching and are cared for by both parents.

The Clapper Rail feeds principally on fiddler crabs and other crustaceans, small snails, and aquatic insects.

AMERICAN COOT, *Fulica americana*

Often called Mud Hen. A ducklike water bird, smaller than a Mallard. Its feet are peculiarly large and are un-webbed, with lobes on all toes. A fairly common migrant, especially in eastern Long Island. The largest numbers appear in November but small numbers may linger in protected waters until frozen out. Now breeding abundantly at the Jamaica Bay Wildlife Refuge, but very rarely elsewhere.

Both sexes black to gray all over, except for bill, edge of inner wing, and feathers under tail, which are white. Immature birds similar but have duller bill, a brownish tinge on back, and lighter underparts. Coots are unusually noisy during the nesting season, uttering a variety of sounds from whistles and cooing notes to loud croaks and chicken-like cackles.

Nest, usually well concealed by tall marsh vegetation, consists of a crude shallow cup of dead reeds and similar plant material, just above water level and near open water. Eggs: 6 to 9, buffy, evenly speckled with black. Incubation: 23 days, by both sexes. Hatching is staggered. While the male broods, the female brings food to the newly hatched chicks and leads the older ones from the nest.

Coots are omnivorous, eating roots, stems, and leaves of aquatic plants, as well as small fish, mollusks, and many aquatic insects. Some of their food is obtained by diving.

SEMIPALMATED PLOVER, *Charadrius semipalmatus*

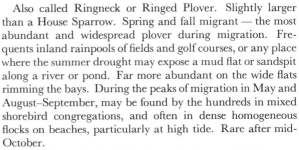

Also called Ringneck or Ringed Plover. Slightly larger than a House Sparrow. Spring and fall migrant — the most abundant and widespread plover during migration. Frequents inland rainpools of fields and golf courses, or any place where the summer drought may expose a mud flat or sandspit along a river or pond. Far more abundant on the wide flats rimming the bays. During the peaks of migration in May and August–September, may be found by the hundreds in mixed shorebird congregations, and often in dense homogeneous flocks on beaches, particularly at high tide. Rare after mid-October.

A short-legged, short-billed shorebird (sexes alike), brownish above (the color of *wet* sand) with white ring around the neck. Underparts white with *one* black band across the breast. Bill orange-yellow with black tip; legs orange-yellow. Call

is a clear musical *chee-wee,* the second note higher. The Piping
Plover, *C. melodus,* which is a summer resident of the outer
beaches, is paler above (the color of *dry* sand) and gives a bell-
like call, *peep-lo,* the first note higher. The Wilson's Plover,
C. wilsonia, which is extremely rare in our area, is somewhat
larger, with a heavy black bill, white line over the eye, and
pinkish legs.

Semipalmated, Piping, and Wilson's Plovers run in short
spurts, then pause to stab the ground, picking up tiny insects
and other crustaceans, their principal food.

KILLDEER, *Charadrius vociferus*

Size of a Robin but with long legs and pointed wings.
Occurs in migration and summer on open fields, golf courses,
and farmlands, as well as in parks, and along the edges of
marshes, rivers, and lakes. One of the first shorebirds to arrive
in spring and among the last to leave in fall with many
wintering in open fields and marshlands.

A long-legged, short-billed plover (sexes alike), brownish
above, with white ring around the neck and a striking orange
rump, and long tail having black, then white, bands around
outer margin. Underparts white with *two* black bands across
breast; central white stripe runs entire length of wing. Very
noisy, with frequent, harsh, high-pitched cries of *killdee, killdee,* or *dee dee dee* repeated very rapidly.

Nests are in such open places as plowed fields, croplands,
golf courses, and gravelly roadsides. The nest is a slight hollow
lined with a few pebbles or bits of grass. Eggs: 4, creamy buff
or brown, heavily spotted or streaked with dark brown and
black, blending so well with their surroundings they are difficult to see. Incubation: 24 to 26 days, by both sexes. The
chicks leave the nest soon after hatching and are cared for by
both parents.

Food is mostly insects of a wide variety, but earthworms
and small aquatic animals are taken.

SPOTTED SANDPIPER, *Actitis macularia*

Between House Sparrow and Robin in size. Summer resident, mid-April to October. Found along rivers and small
streams, around lakes and ponds, and along the marshy margins of tidal creeks and bays. Does not flock like many other
shorebirds. Never very wary.

Sexes alike. Spring birds have olive-brown upperparts and
white underparts with round, black spots. Bill pinkish at
base. Fall birds lack spots but have a white shoulder mark.
Identified at any time by the habitual teetering of the body.
In flight, the birds show a double white wing stripe and white-
spotted outer tail feathers. The wings appear to vibrate rather

than flap, seem stiff and down-bowed. When flushed, the birds usually skim in a wide arc, close to water, soon alighting again. Song, a sweet *prret-weet-weet-weet-weet*, or a sharp *peet-weet*, often given in flight and sometimes heard on spring nights.

Nest is a depression in ground, lined with grasses and fine materials, usually near water. Often placed near vegetation at edge of open beach or rocks. Eggs: 4, buff, spotted and blotched with dark brown. Incubation: 21 days, by male. Downy young run soon after hatching. When approached they squat, and are almost impossible to find. They can fly when 10 to 16 days old.

Food mostly insects and small crustaceans picked up on the water's edge.

GREATER YELLOWLEGS, *Totanus melanoleucus*

Common spring and fall migrant, usually seen between early April and June, and between mid-July and early November, but a few individuals may be observed in any month of the year. Found in typical shorebird habitat, fresh as well as salt, wherever mud flats afford feeding grounds.

A large wader, close to a Robin in body bulk but appearing bigger because of its slender neck, long bill, and long stiltlike legs. Sexes alike. Dark grayish above, flecked and barred with white, whitish below, finely marked with black on neck and breast. Legs bright yellow, bill black, long, and slightly up-turned. In flight, shows unstriped dark wings, white rump, and white tail finely barred with black. The long legs trail behind squarish tail. Call is a loud, ringing *kew, kew-kew,* the first note highest, often given in flight. The very similar Lesser Yellowlegs, *T. flavipes,* is smaller, with shorter, straight, and slender bill. Call similar to Greater's, but of two *kews* only.

The Greater Yellowlegs feeds while wading in shallow water, taking its food from the surface or submerging the head to probe the muddy bottom. Often wades into deeper waters, where it swims buoyantly. Eats many small fish, insects, and other aquatic animals.

The Greater Yellowlegs walks gracefully with long strides, periodically bobbing the head, like a mechanical toy. It is taller than most of the other shorebirds with which it associates.

SHORT-BILLED DOWITCHER,
Limnodromus griseus

Robin size, but its snipe-like bill and plump build make it seem larger. On a beach it is medium-sized when compared to the little "peeps" (such as the Semipalmated Sandpiper) and the taller Willets and Whimbrels. A common migrant along the coastal waters, reaching greatest numbers in May and July to October, with maximum abundance on Long Island and the nearby New Jersey tidal flats in late July and again in early September. Less common along Long Island Sound and very rare away from saltwater. A swift-flying, gregarious species, often mingling with other shorebirds, but frequently found in dense flocks of its own kind. Under optimum conditions, 1000 or more may be counted in a single day.

Sexes alike. Spring birds have upperparts dark brown streaked with buffy, except lower back and rump which are white; underparts washed with cinnamon-red. Tail white, with faint bars. Fall birds less brownish (almost gray) above, light gray to white below with occasional traces of cinnamon. Bill dusky and legs green. In flight, the white on back, rump, and tail make a conspicuous vertical streak that readily iden-tifies the dowitcher. Call is a soft, liquid *pheu-pheu,* or *pheu-pheu-pheu,* with a rising inflection.

Food consists mainly of marine invertebrates, such as clam worms, obtained by rapid, persistent probing in mud, often in shallow water. Sometimes dowitchers wade in water up to their bellies and submerge their heads when probing deeply. When not feeding, flocks may be seen sleeping or resting, each bird balanced on one leg with head tucked under the back feathers.

SEMIPALMATED SANDPIPER, *Ereunetes pusillus*

About the size of a House Sparrow. The commonest "peep" — one of several species of small, scampering sand-pipers that appear as migrants in spring and fall. Also the most abundant shorebird, usually seen from early May to mid-June, and from late July through mid-October, though it has been recorded every month except January and Feb-ruary. Found in such typical shorebird habitat as tidal pools, mud flats, beaches, and sandbars; in lesser numbers along the banks of ponds and streams, wherever insects, crustaceans, and other minute animal life may be gleaned from the mud or sand.

One of our smallest shorebirds, with a fairly short black bill, stouter at base, and black legs and feet. Sexes alike. Spring adults are dark gray-brown above, the feathers margined with gray, white below with faint streaks on sides. Immature birds in late summer have buffy tips to feathers and no streaks below. When in the hand, the Semipalmated Sandpiper shows webbing between the front toes. The shorebird most easily confused with this species is the less common and slightly smaller Least Sandpiper, *Erolia minutilla,* whose bill is slender throughout, legs and feet greenish, and over-all ap-pearance brownish, with distinct streaks below. Call of the

Semipalmated is a loud *churk,* also a fainter *tee-in,* usually given in flight.

The Semipalmated is remarkably tame. From its breeding grounds in the North American arctic, it migrates many hundreds of miles southward to its wintering grounds, which extend from the Gulf Coast to southern South America.

HERRING GULL, *Larus argentatus*

A big, bulky bird 2 feet in length; graceful in flight on long wings. The most ubiquitous bird, seen soaring high over Manhattan, following fishing boats at sea, milling by the thousands over garbage dumps. Common at all seasons and even grossly abundant in winter. Nests along the south shore beaches of Long Island.

Adults (sexes alike) white except for gray wings and back, and black wing tips spotted with white. Bill yellow with red spot. Legs pink. First-year immatures dark brown, appearing almost black in the distance; second-year birds, intermediate between first-year and adult, showing increased white on body, gray on wings, but with dark tail and black-tipped bill. Calls include loud screams and mewing sounds. The smaller Ring-billed Gull, *L. delawarensis,* is common in all seasons, but does not breed here. Adults have dark ring around bill and yellow-green legs. Immatures have a prominent, narrow, black band at tip of tail. Calls resemble Herring Gull's but are higher-pitched.

The Herring Gull breeds in colonies. Nest is on the ground, made of dead grasses, weed stalks, and other debris. Eggs: 3, bluish or brownish, spotted and blotched with brown and gray. Incubation: 28 days, by both sexes. Both parents feed the chicks on regurgitated food. Young are able to fly in about 6 weeks.

Herring and Ring-billed Gulls are notorious but nonetheless useful scavengers, taking most any food, alive or dead, available at beaches, garbage dumps, and picnic areas.

COMMON TERN, *Sterna hirundo*

A slender, dainty bird, longer than Robin with long pointed wings, deeply forked tail, and swallow-like flight. Common summer resident, found anywhere around saltwater but abundant along the south shore of Long Island and in Peconic Bay.

Adults (sexes alike) are white, with gray wings and back, dusky wing-tips, black cap, orange-red bill tipped with black, and orange-red feet. Adults in fall and immatures have black bill and white forehead. The call is a husky, down-slurred *kee-aaar.* Alarm is a hard *kik-kik-kik.* Other white terns seen in summer are the similarly sized Roseate Tern, *S. dougallii,* with a long, streaming, deeply forked tail and a low-pitched call, *aaak,* and the half-sized Least Tern, *S. albifrons,* with white forehead, yellow bill and legs, and a rasping call, *cher-eep.*

Common Terns nest in colonies on sandy beaches. Nest is a depression in sand, sometimes sparsely lined with shells and pebbles. Eggs: 2 or 3, buff or brown, heavily spotted with dark brown. Incubation: 23 to 25 days, by both sexes. Downy chicks leave the nest in about 5 days. Both parents bring small fish held crosswise in their beaks, and these the chicks swallow whole. Young terns fly when about a month old.

Food consists almost entirely of small fish, obtained by diving into the water.

ROCK DOVE, *Columba livia*

More often called Pigeon. Although normally ignored by bird watchers, it is typical of the metropolitan scene. Found in flocks from ten to hundreds throughout New York City and suburbs, preferring parks and squares wherever a few trees may afford a perch. In the city it lives mainly on human largess, but in suburban and rural areas it is independent and wild, feeding in corn fields, garbage dumps, and ocean beaches alike.

Hardy, prolific, adaptable, the Pigeon is descended from the wild Rock Dove of Europe and Asia, domesticated centuries ago. In its many plumage variations it shows the evidence of the admixture of strains developed over the years by pigeon fanciers. The sexes are indistinguishable. Pigeons are normally slate-gray with green and purplish iridescence on head and neck, but they are occasionally tan-colored, or black, or pied black and white. Their call is the familiar gurgled cooing sound, many times repeated.

Breeds almost year round, on sheltered ledges of cliffs (its natural habitat) and eaves of buildings, in belfries, under bridges, and so on. The nest is a messy assemblage of debris, just barely cupped. Eggs: 2, white. Incubation: 17 days, mainly by female. Young are fed by both parents on regurgitated food and fly in about 5 weeks.

The food preferred is grain, but Pigeons will eat seeds, peanuts, bread, and some fruit, often freeloading at bird feeders. Around garbage dumps they scavenge like gulls.

MOURNING DOVE, *Zenaidura macroura*

Slightly larger than a Robin. Common summer resident in all but densely urban areas, wintering in increasing numbers as wards of feeding stations. Prefers open dry areas such as open fields, estate grounds, parks, and golf courses, with trees in the vicinity. Often seen perching on utility wires

along highways. The Mourning Dove occurs in pairs during spring and summer but gathers in flocks by fall. It often roosts with Robins and Common Grackles in coniferous groves.

This bird has a long pointed tail with white tips on the outer feathers, conspicuous when it spreads the tail to alight. The neck is rather long and the head seems small. Tan all over, darker above, with a black cheek spot. Sexes alike. The flight is rapid and direct, accompanied by a whistling of the wings. Walks with dainty steps. In spring it performs a sailing flight with down-bowed wings. The bird is named for its mournful call — *auoo-oooo-oooo-oo* — which is mistaken for an owl's by many beginners.

Nest is a loose platform of twigs, occasionally on ground but usually 10 to 25 feet from ground in a deciduous or coniferous tree. Eggs: 2, white. Incubation: 14 to 15 days, by both sexes. Young are fed on regurgitated seeds in white liquid ("pigeon's milk") formed in crop of male and female. They stay in nest 13 to 15 days. Two broods.

Food, consisting of seeds and grain, obtained mostly on ground.

YELLOW-BILLED CUCKOO, *Coccyzus americanus*

A slender, long-tailed bird about the size of a Robin. A fairly common summer resident, from the first of May through September. The closely related species, the Black-billed Cuckoo, *C. erythropthalmus,* is also a summer resident but apparently not as common. Both species occur in open deciduous woodlands, in orchards, and in shade trees and thickets along streams and roads. They are often overlooked because of their retiring habits.

Both sexes grayish brown above, with reddish brown on wings (noticeable in flight); white below, with long tail feathers showing *broad* white tips. Bill is slightly downcurved, the upper mandible black and lower yellow. The Black-billed Cuckoo has *narrow* white tips on tail, bill wholly black, red eye-ring, and no reddish brown on wings. Song is a continuous, unmusical series of *kuk*'s, more slowly given toward end. Song of the Black-billed is similar but with *kuk*'s in groups of 3 or 4 rather than in continuous series, thus: *kuk-kuk-kuk, kuk-kuk-kuk-kuk,* etc.

The nest of the Yellow-billed Cuckoo is a loosely built platform of twigs, placed in a thickly foliaged tree, shrub, or vine, seldom more than 10 feet from ground. Eggs: 2 or 3, pale greenish blue. Incubation: about 14 days, by both sexes. Young probably stay in nest no longer than 9 days.

Cuckoos feed on tent caterpillars in large numbers when abundant. Also eat other caterpillars and insects, and occasionally berries.

SCREECH OWL, *Otus asio*

The length of a Robin but seemingly much heavier because of its fluffy plumage. Permanent resident — our only fairly common owl — but decreasing around New York City because it shuns heavily populated areas. Prefers woodlands, orchards, dense-foliaged groves, but may appear almost anywhere, even on rooftops during its nightly hunting.

The only small owl with ear tufts. Adults and immatures alike with two color phases, red and gray, which have no relation to age or sex. In red phase, upperparts predominantly reddish brown, streaked with black and buffy white; underparts white, streaked with black and barred with reddish brown. In gray phase, markings essentially the same, except that gray replaces reddish brown. Its call is a prolonged, quavering, descending whistle, with a plaintive quality.

Nest is usually in a tree cavity, such as a rotted-out knothole or a woodpecker hole. Has no nesting material. Eggs: 4 to 5, white. Incubation: about 26 days. Young leave the nest after about a month. Nesting starts in late March or early April.

Prey consists of a variety of small animals ranging from night-flying insects such as moths to earthworms, frogs, birds, mice, and bats. Like other owls, it can be located in a grove by searching the ground for fresh pellets — the wads of fur, bones, and other undigested matter cast up while roosting — and then inspecting the tree overhead for the bird.

COMMON NIGHTHAWK, *Chordeiles minor*

About the size of a Robin, appearing larger in flight because of its long wings and tail. Local summer resident from early May to late September, breeding in scattered towns in Westchester, Rockland, Putnam, Orange, and Suffolk Counties; absent elsewhere except in migration, when it may appear commonly almost anywhere.

Both sexes black, heavily barred and marked with white, gray, and buff, the male with a white bar on tail. The Nighthawk is easily recognized by its erratic flight and the white band crossing each wing. Flaps with deep wingbeats, now fluttering upward after an insect, or gliding with wings held in a V. Active at dusk, during the day, and sometimes at night. When not flying, perches on the ground, or lengthwise on a tree limb, where it is difficult to see. The call is a loud nasal *peeent*. During courtship season, also makes a twanging boom, caused by vibration of wing feathers as the bird swoops up after one of its spectacular earthward dives.

No nest is built, the eggs being laid on bare gravel, in a pasture, on the ground in burned woodland, or on a flat rooftop. Eggs: 2, creamy, heavily speckled or blotched with black, gray, or lavender. Incubation: 19 days, by female. Both parents care for young, which fly at about 3 weeks of age.

Food, captured on the wing, consists of insects — flying ants, moths, beetles, mosquitoes, etc.

CHIMNEY SWIFT, *Chaetura pelagica*

Smaller than a House Sparrow, has tiny feet and bill. Common summer resident everywhere except in densely urban areas, arriving in early May and departing in mid-September. Especially common in suburban counties and around farm buildings. In evening during migration large numbers of Swifts may collect over a chimney, finally spiraling into it, like smoke in reverse, to roost for the night.

Easily recognized by its sooty-brown color (appears black against the sky), streamlined body, apparent lack of tail, and long, narrow wings. It seems ever on the wing and seldom rests anywhere, except inside chimneys, hollow trees, and abandoned buildings, where it clings to vertical surfaces. Frequently several Swifts wheel about together with rapid wingbeats that may appear to be alternate, or glide on stiff down-bowed wings, or on wings held in a V. Sometimes they may fly a perfect formation. Their chippering notes are often heard high in the sky, though the birds themselves are scarcely visible.

Nest, built by both sexes, is a cup of twigs, cemented together and stuck to the inside of a chimney by saliva from the bird's mouth. Eggs: 4 to 5, white. Incubation: 19 to 21 days, by both sexes. Young are fed by regurgitation during first week; remain in nest for 2 weeks or more, and take first flight from chimney in about a month.

Swifts feed entirely on insects caught on the wing.

RUBY-THROATED HUMMINGBIRD, *Archilochus colubris*

Our smallest bird, measuring less than 4 inches. Uncommon summer resident from late April to mid-September. Occurs about flower gardens, woodland clearings, and edges of woods. Sometimes seen migrating in fall along the edge of the ocean surf.

Both sexes metallic green above and white below — the male with a red throat (appears black in some lights) — and with a long, needlelike bill. The Hummingbird is usually seen hovering in front of flowers, its wings a blur, soon darting away and out of sight. Occasionally mistaken for a large clear-winged moth. Notes are harsh clicking or buzzing sounds. The hum produced by the wings in flight gives the bird its name. In spring the male engages in a courtship flight, diving at the female with tail spread, or swinging about in precise arcs.

Nest, built by the female, is a tiny, exquisite cup of plant down, bud scales, and lichens, bound with spider silk and saddled on the limb of a tree or shrub. Eggs: 2, white. Incubation: 16 days, by female. The young remain in the nest about 2 weeks. Female feeds them by regurgitation, poking her bill down their throats.

The Hummingbird feeds on nectar by probing into flowers, and may take sap flowing from sapsucker borings. Also darts after insects on the wing. It can be attracted to houses by vials of sweetened water colored red.

BELTED KINGFISHER, *Megaceryle alcyon*

Somewhat bigger than a Robin. Summer resident, arriving in mid-March and leaving by mid-November, with a few scattered individuals lingering into winter where there is open water. Found around freshwater ponds, streams, and reservoirs, usually in isolated pairs.

This stub-tailed, large-headed bird is easily recognized by its bushy double crest, dull blue upperparts, white throat and underparts, and banded breast. The female has russet on the sides, extending across the breast to form a second band. The large, straight, pointed bill seems too big for the bird. The Kingfisher shows uneven shallow wingbeats in flight, typically swooping up to alight on an exposed perch over water. The call, often uttered in flight, is a loud harsh rattle.

Nests in a chamber at the end of a long 3- to 6-foot burrow, excavated by the pair, in a bank usually near water. Eggs: 6 to 7, white. Laid on bare sand in the chamber. Incubation: 23 to 24 days, by both sexes. Young remain in the burrow for about a month, where they are brought food by both parents.

Food consists mostly of small fish, but butterflies, beetles, and crayfish are sometimes taken. Each fish is caught by plunging into water, the bird hovering for some time beforehand. The fish is taken to a perch and swallowed whole, headfirst. The bird's small feet play no part in fishing.

YELLOW-SHAFTED FLICKER, *Colaptes auratus*

Larger than a Robin. Summer resident (mid-April to late October), wintering occasionally in protected woodlands. Often seen migrating in fall by the thousands, particularly along the south shore beaches. Nests in suburban and rural areas, city parks, and cemeteries. Often seen feeding on suburban lawns.

Both sexes are brownish, spotted below and barred above with black, and have a black crescent on the upper breast and a red nape patch. The male and juveniles of both sexes have a black "mustache." When the Flicker bounds through the air, it shows yellow wing linings and a white rump. A familiar call is its loud rapidly repeated call, *wick, wick, wick, wick, wick,* etc. Other calls include a down-slurred *keeyer* and a subdued *flick, aflick, aflick.* In the spring it often drums noisily on hollow stubs, metal gutters, and tin roofs. Courtship involves a lively dance in which two or more bob and jerk back and forth with tails spread.

Nest is usually in a cavity, excavated by both sexes, in a dead or dying tree, 4 to 40 feet above ground, but sometimes it is in a nest box. Eggs: 6 to 9, glossy white. Incubation: 11 to 12 days, by both sexes. Nestlings are fed by regurgitation, leave the nest in about 26 days.

Food consists largely of ants, taken while the bird hops on the ground, driving its bill into ant tunnels. Also a variety of other insects and much wild fruit.

DOWNY WOODPECKER, *Dendrocopos pubescens*

About the size of a House Sparrow. Permanent resident, only slightly migratory, but seemingly more abundant in October. Prefers deciduous woodlands but found in urban areas where trees remain, occasionally even in Manhattan gardens. Usually very tame, coming to suburban feeders in winter.

Both sexes are white below and black above, with white patches, spots, and stripes. Outer tail. feathers white with black spots. Male has a single red nape patch. The flight is bounding, the birds appearing stubby-tailed on the wing. Calls include a dry *pick* and a descending rattle or whinny. During courtship both birds posture, like mechanical dolls, calling *wick, wick, wick wick.* The Hairy Woodpecker, *D. villosus,* is almost a duplicate except that it is one-third larger, lacks spots on tail, has a proportionately longer, heavier, larger bill, and a divided red nape patch. Also a permanent resident, but it shuns urban areas and is far less common on Long Island.

Both sexes of the Downy help drill the nest cavity, usually in a dead limb, 8 to 50 feet above ground. Eggs: 4 or 5, white. Incubation: 12 days, by both sexes. The nestlings soon clamor for food, coming to the nest hole to meet the parent.

Food consists mostly of insects, such as ants and beetle larvae, and some fruit. Much of the insect food is obtained by boring into dead wood with the bill or chipping off flakes of bark. The long tongue secures the food.

EASTERN KINGBIRD, *Tyrannus tyrannus*

Slightly smaller than a Robin. Widely distributed summer resident (early May to mid-September) except in urban and densely populated suburban areas. Prefers open country, where it often perches on wires, posts, and dead stubs between its aerial sallies for insects. The Kingbird is notoriously aggressive, never hesitating to attack hawks, crows, and other birds many times its size. Occasionally it will fearlessly strike its foe.

This flycatcher (sexes alike) is blackish above and white below and easily recognized by the broad white band at the end of its tail, which shows plainly in flight, and fluttering wingbeats. A noisy bird, it seems to be chronically angry, scolding with loud grating notes, *zee-zeeb,* and hurried, shrill chatter, *kit-kit-kitter kitter, kitter, kip.*

Nests placed 4 to 30 feet from the ground, usually in lone trees (apple trees favored), but sometimes on stumps and fence posts; a bulky structure of twigs and plant stems, lined with grasses and plant down. Eggs: 3 to 4, white, spotted with dark brown and gray. Incubation: 13 days, by female. Both parents feed the young, which stay in nest until 15 or more days old.

About 90 per cent of the food consists of insects, chiefly flying forms that are caught on the wing; the remainder of small fruits and seeds.

EASTERN PHOEBE, *Sayornis phoebe*

Slightly larger than a House Sparrow, but much thinner. Fairly common summer resident in less urbanized areas, preferring the vicinity of water — the banks of streams and low, flooded woodlands. Our earliest flycatcher to arrive in spring (late March) and last to leave in fall (early November), with an occasional bird lingering into January. Most individuals pass the winter from southeastern United States to southern Mexico.

Though colored — gray-brown above and dusky white below — with no conspicuous field marks, this flycatcher (sexes alike) can be quickly recognized when perched by its habit of jerking or wagging its tail up and down and sidewise. Unlike the Eastern Wood Pewee, *Contopus virens,* and the smaller Least Flycatcher, *Empidonax minimus,* the Phoebe has a black bill, head darker than the back, and no wing bars. A further aid to identification is the emphatic, two-syllabled call, *phoe-bee* (not to be confused with the Black-capped Chickadee's *pee-bee,* which is a plaintive whistle).

Nest placed on almost any jutting surface — beam, window frame, bridge girder, ledge shelf — that has overhead shelter; a cup made of mosses and mud, lined with grasses and other soft materials. Eggs: usually 5, white. Incubation: 16 days, by female. Both parents feed the young, which stay in the nest 16 days. Two broods raised per year.

Ninety per cent of the food is animal matter, chiefly insects. Plant matter consists of berries and other small fruits and seeds.

HORNED LARK, *Eremophila alpestris*

A ground bird, slightly larger than a House Sparrow, preferring open country. There are two kinds (but not different species) of Horned Larks in our region: the Northern, a common winter visitant (October to April), frequently in flocks over fields and beaches; and the Prairie, a less common breeding resident on Long Island, where it is one of our earliest nesters, sometimes laying eggs in late February.

Horned Larks (sexes alike) are mainly grayish to pinkish brown above and white below with a black tail, conspicuous in flight; black patch across forehead extending into "horns"; black band from bill to eye, extended on the side of the head to form a "mustache"; another black band across the breast. The Northern form has the black bands separated by yellow, the Prairie by white. Horned Larks seldom perch in trees; they walk rather than hop, and have an undulating flight. Their call note is a high-pitched *whitzurrit;* the song a series of tinkling sounds, often in flight high overhead.

The Prairie Horned Lark nests on the ground, in short grass on airfields, golf courses, even along margins of parkways; nest of grass, lined with plant down, feathers, and other soft materials. Eggs: 3 to 5, drab, speckled with brown. Incubation: 11 days, by female. Both parents feed the young, which stay in nest 9 to 11 days.

Eighty per cent of food is plant matter, chiefly seeds; the rest consists of various insects.

TREE SWALLOW, *Iridoprocne bicolor*

Slightly smaller than a House Sparrow. Widely distributed summer resident, late March to October, except in urban areas. Frequents meadows, marshes, the edges of ponds, and other places not far from water over which it can feed on insects. Gathers in flocks soon after nesting, often lining up on wires by the hundreds, side by side, separated evenly by short spaces. By late September, Tree Swallows, in congregations totaling thousands, may be seen over our outer beaches and salt marshes, passing in spectacular mass flights. An occasional individual lingers into December.

Tail slightly forked. Adults (sexes alike) are glossy blue-black above (with deep greenish reflections in some lights), pure white below. Juveniles are sooty brown above with a faint breastband on very white breast. Vocal sounds are warbling twitters, a *tsip-prrup-prrup,* many times repeated.

Nests placed in natural cavities, woodpecker holes, and bird boxes, usually not far from water or wet places; made of grasses and other plant materials and lined with white feathers. Eggs: 3 to 5, white. Incubation: 13 to 16 days, by both sexes. Both parents feed the young, which stay in the nest 16 or more days.

About 80 per cent of the food is animal matter, mainly insects flying low over open water or wet places; the remainder consists of seeds and berries, taken especially when insect food is scarce during cold weather.

BARN SWALLOW, *Hirundo rustica*

Longer than a House Sparrow, but much more slender. Summer resident (mid-April to late September) in less urban areas, preferring abandoned buildings, barns, boathouses, etc. Abundant in fall, often with other swallows in large flocks. Like other swallows, they migrate mainly by day.

The only swallow with a long, deeply forked tail. Adults (sexes alike) have forehead, chin, and throat reddish brown, top of head and back glossy steel-blue, breast with blackish band, rest of breast and underparts pale cinnamon, inner margins of tail feathers white. Juveniles have nearly square tails and are lighter below. Vocal sounds are liquid, frequently repeated twitters, *kwik-kwik, wit, wit,* and an emphatic *kittic* when disturbed or excited. The Cliff Swallow, *Petrochelidon pyrrhonota,* an uncommon migrant, can be readily distinguished from the Barn Swallow by square tail and light reddish rump. It nests rarely in our area.

Barn Swallow nests are in or on barns and permanently deserted buildings, or under bridges, plastered onto either a vertical or a jutting horizontal surface with overhead shelter; made of mud mixed with dried grass and lined with fine grasses and feathers. Eggs: 3 to 6, white, spotted with brown. Incubation: 13 to 15 days, by female. Both parents feed the young, which stay in nest about 18 days. Two broods raised per year.

Practically all food consists of animal matter, chiefly flying insects.

BLUE JAY, *Cyanocitta cristata*

Larger than a Robin. Noisy, aggressive resident, favoring deciduous woodlands, particularly oaks. Frequents city parks, suburban communities, and more rural areas. Common migrant, often abundant on flight days in October.

Adults (sexes alike) have conspicuous crests and strong bills. Above grayish blue, the wings and long tail strikingly marked with bright blue, black, and white. Underparts grayish white. A noticeable black collar runs from hind neck to upper chest. Juveniles similar to adults, but grayer. The Blue Jay's usual call is a piercing *jay, jay,* but it produces a variety of other sounds, ranging from bell-like *tull-ull* to raucous chatters. It is also remarkably capable as a imitator, especially of hawks. Groups of jays with much commotion will often mob an owl found perched in daylight.

Nests placed in densely foliaged trees, usually in crotches

near trunks, 5 to 50 feet from the ground. A bulky structure of weed stalks, twigs, rootlets, and strips of bark, lined with finer materials. Eggs: 3 to 6, pale gray-green, heavily marked with brown and gray spots. Incubation: 16 to 18 days, by both sexes. Both parents feed the young, which stay in the nest 17 to 21 days.

Omnivorous, eating almost any kind of food. The Blue Jay is sometimes disliked because of its tendency to monopolize feeders and its habit of taking the eggs and young of smaller birds.

COMMON CROW, *Corvus brachyrhynchos*

Larger than any blackbird, being about 20 inches long. Widely distributed permanent resident but far less common than formerly, owing to "urban sprawl." More abundant in open country and near water. Migrates in numbers through our region, in part along ridges. In winter, congregates nightly in large roosts, the birds coming in all directions from distances up to 50 miles. The Crow is one of the most sagacious and adaptable of birds.

Crows are completely black and the sexes identical in size. The Common Crow's usual call is the familiar *ca-aw*. The smaller Fish Crow, *C. ossifragus* (17 inches long), is an uncommon summer resident, frequenting woodlands near water. It is best distinguished by its calls — a low two-noted *aaah-ah* and a short hoarse *kaak*.

Common Crows begin nesting in late March, choosing tall trees from 18 to 60 feet above ground. Nests are made of sticks, grasses, strips of bark, leaves, rags, mud, etc., rough-appearing outwardly, but neatly lined. Eggs: 3 to 6, pale bluish or olive-green, with irregular blotches of various browns and shades of gray. Incubation: 15 to 18 days, by both sexes. Young stay in nest 4 to 5 weeks.

Omnivorous, eating almost any food alive or dead: eggs, young birds, mammals, reptiles, fish, insects, and carrion; seeds, nuts, acorns, grain, sprouting corn, and fruits. The Crow's reputation as a depredator has been greatly exaggerated.

BLACK-CAPPED CHICKADEE, *Parus atricapillus*

Smaller than a House Sparrow. Widely distributed permanent resident, occurring in city parks, suburbia, and nearly all wooded areas. In fall, winter, and spring, many individuals are inclined to rove in small groups that forage through the trees, often hanging upside down to feed. Common at feeders and quite fearless. With patience a person may induce some individuals to feed from his hand.

Sexes alike, with top of head and throat black, cheeks white, rest of upperparts grayish, and underparts grayish white, with

pale buffy wash on flanks. Bill short. Juveniles like adults. The Chickadee's familiar call is an animated, distinctly uttered *chick-a-dee-dee-dee.* It also gives, most frequently in the spring, a high, plaintive whistle, *pee-bee,* the first note higher.

Nest is in a cavity dug by the female in a rotted tree or stump, or in a deserted woodpecker hole, or bird box, 3 to 6 feet above the ground, occasionally higher, made of feathers, hair, moss, and other soft materials. Eggs: normally 6 to 8, white lightly speckled with reddish brown. Incubation: 12 days, by both sexes. Both parents feed the young, which stay in the nest about 2 weeks.

Food consists of spiders and a wide variety of insects (including their eggs and larvae) injurious to trees. In winter it will take seeds, suet, peanut butter, and other feeder fare. In its tireless search for insects, the Chickadee covers all parts of a tree.

WHITE-BREASTED NUTHATCH, *Sitta carolinensis*

The size of a House Sparrow. Permanent resident wherever deciduous woodlands of any size remain. In winter may appear almost anywhere — parks, suburban gardens, orchards, tree-lined streets, etc. — but is never abundant.

Adults (sexes alike) have a black cap, blue-gray back, white face, and white underparts with rusty flanks. The juveniles are similar. Red-breasted Nuthatches, *S. canadensis,* which are fairly common though irregular winter visitants (September to May), are slightly smaller, with a black line through the eye and cinnamon underparts. Nuthatches are readily distinguished from other small birds by their habit of creeping down tree trunks headfirst as they search for insect food. The White-breasted's common call is a nasal *yank-yank,* the Red-breasted's is *ya-ya-ya,* more nasal and higher-pitched.

White-breasted's nests are occasionally in bird boxes, but usually in tree cavities — woodpecker holes or natural crevices, 10 to 60 feet from the ground; made of shredded bark, mosses, grasses, leaves, and lined with hair and feathers. Eggs: normally 7 or 8, white, evenly spotted with reddish brown. Incubation: 12 days, by both sexes. Both parents feed the young, which stay in the nest about 14 days.

Food consists of animal matter, such as insects, their eggs and larvae, and spiders, and various seeds and small nuts, which are often carried off and hidden in crevices of bark.

HOUSE WREN, *Troglodytes aedon*

Smaller than a House Sparrow. Summer resident (May to October) in suburban and rural areas, frequenting gardens and parks, roadsides, and the edge of woodlands.

Both sexes gray-brown all over but paler beneath; wings and tail finely barred with black. The House Wren is an energetic mite, distinguished less by its appearance than its song — a loud and rapid bubbling of short duration, falling in pitch at the end. It is given almost incessantly in the spring and early summer. The call is a grating chatter. The slightly smaller Winter Wren, *T. troglodytes,* which is an uncommon winter visitant frequenting thickets and brushpiles, has a very short tail often cocked well over its back, a whitish line over the eye, and dark, barred underparts.

The House Wren nests in any convenient cavity, from bird-houses to tin cans, usually within 10 feet of the ground. Male may build several nests, but only one is rebuilt later by his mate and used. Nest bulky, of twigs and debris, lined with feathers. Eggs: 6 to 8, white, heavily speckled with reddish brown. Incubation: 13 to 14 days, by both sexes. Young spend 2 weeks in nest. Two broods raised per year.

The food, gathered in shrubs and trees or on the ground, consists of insects — bugs, beetles, grasshoppers, and caterpillars.

The House Wren has the habit of puncturing the eggs of other birds. Notwithstanding, it is actually a persistent pest destroyer about gardens, as well as a source of amusement when it cocks up its tail in excitement or depresses it while singing.

CATBIRD, *Dumetella carolinensis*

Slightly smaller than a Robin. Widely distributed summer resident, late April to October, with occasional birds lingering in sheltered thickets into December. Prefers brushy areas, briar patches, hedges, deciduous thickets, and shrub-bordered gardens.

Both sexes dark gray all over except for a black cap and chestnut patch under the tail. The species is named for its mewing, catlike call. Sings from low bushes or trees, or from an exposed perch near dense cover. Song is a long series of musical or harsh phrases, varying in pitch and separated by pauses. Sometimes the calls or songs are imitations of other birds. Difficult to see in dense vegetation, the Catbird can sometimes be attracted to the open by squeaking noises and will respond with a low *chut.*

Nest placed in bushes, garden shrubs, or dense conifers, 2 to 10 feet above the ground; made by both sexes of twigs, bark, and weed stems, lined with rootlets, forming a bulky structure. Eggs: 4, glossy greenish blue and unmarked. Incubation: 12 to 13 days, by both sexes. Both parents feed the young, which stay in the nest 10 or more days.

The Catbird often feeds on the ground, rustling the leaves in its search for food. It eats many kinds of insects and spiders, also several kinds of wild and cultivated berries. When it hops on the ground, the wings are often dropped and the long rounded tail appears loosely attached.

BROWN THRASHER, *Toxostoma rufum*

The size of a Robin, but slimmer. Summer resident, except in dense woodlands and densely urban areas, from late April until mid-October. A few linger into winter. Found along woodland borders and dry open areas where there are bushes and scattered low trees.

The bright reddish-brown upperparts, the underparts conspicuously streaked (not spotted) with black, and long tail identify this bird. Its bill curves downward, and the alert yellow eye can be seen at close range. Sexes similar. Usually a skulker in thickets and shrubs. Song, usually given from the top of a high tree, is a long series of loud and varied phrases, many of them repeated. Some phrases are rasping, others musical. Occasionally imitates other birds. Alarm note is a harsh *smack*.

Nest built in low shrub, brushpile, or sometimes on ground; made by both sexes of twigs, leaves, and rootlets to form a large structure. Eggs: 4 or 5, bluish or white, finely speckled with reddish brown. Incubation: 12 to 13 days, by both sexes. Both parents feed the young, which leave the nest in 9 to 12 days. Parent birds are fearless at the nest, often flying at intruders and clawing or pecking them.

Thrashers feed mostly on the ground, where they swing the bill from side to side, scattering the leaves. They walk, hop, or run, sometimes pursuing insects on foot. Besides eating insects — especially beetles, caterpillars, crickets, and ants — they take some wild fruits.

ROBIN, *Turdus migratorius*

This well-known thrush, 10 inches long, is a summer resident throughout suburbia and the more rural areas, also in the larger city parks. It arrives early in March and leaves by mid-November. Although the "first Robin" is a traditional sign of spring, a considerable number winter in sheltered places where food is available.

Male gray above and brick-red below, with black head, yellow bill, and black-streaked throat. Female paler. Juveniles faintly reddish below with prominent spots. The familiar early morning and evening song or carol consists of rich, warbled phrases, uttered in rapid succession. The calls are numerous, some loud and ringing, others whispered.

Nest placed in a tree, either in a crotch or on a horizontal branch, or on protected, jutting surfaces of man-made structures, usually 5 to 15 feet above ground; made by female, of coarse grasses and other materials, cemented with mud, forming a deep, smooth cup, lined with fine grasses. Eggs: usually 4, plain blue. Incubation: 12 to 13 days, by female. Both parents feed the young, which stay in the nest about 2 weeks. Two or three broods raised per year.

Food includes wild and cultivated fruits, sumac seeds, beetles, caterpillars, and particularly earthworms. Robins hunt earthworms by running or hopping, periodically stopping to cock an eye or ear. Once located, the worm is quickly pulled from its burrow.

WOOD THRUSH, *Hylocichla mustelina*

Smaller than a Robin. Summer resident from early May to mid-October. Prefers the more moist deciduous and mixed woodlands, but frequently occurs in heavily shaded, undisturbed spots in parks and suburban gardens. Primarily a bird of the forest floor and understory.

Sexes alike. Reddish brown above, brighter on the head and neck, with a prominent eye-ring; white below, marked (unlike any other thrush) with *round black spots.* Much heavier-bodied than the Hermit Thrush, *H. guttata,* which lacks the eye-ring and has a reddish-brown tail and indistinct spots on the breast. (The Hermit is a resident only in the pine barrens of Suffolk County, and the higher altitudes of our northern counties.) The Wood Thrush's song is a series of clear-toned melodious phrases of 3 to 5 distinct notes, some high-pitched and others rich and deep, with distinct pauses between phrases. Alarm note is a loud, sharp *pick-pick-pick-pick.*

Nests placed in a crotch of a small tree or on a horizontal lower limb of a large tree, 5 to 20 feet from the ground; a deep cup of grasses, long strips of bark, paper, string, and leaves; with an inner mud wall, lined with rootlets and other fine materials. Eggs: 3 to 4, pale blue. Incubation: 12 to 13 days, by female. Both parents feed the young, which stay in the nest about 2 weeks.

Spiders and various insects, and to a lesser extent vegetable matter — berries, other small fruits, and seeds — constitute most of the food.

GOLDEN-CROWNED KINGLET, *Regulus satrapa*

A tiny, lively midget, smaller than a House Sparrow. Next to the Ruby-throated Hummingbird our smallest bird. Fairly common migrant (April, October, and November) and unpredictable winter visitant — in some winters it is relatively common, in others virtually absent. Frequents woodlands and coniferous groves, foraging in small bands, often in company with Black-capped Chickadees,

Brown Creepers, and nuthatches. In feeding, may forsake
the higher branches of trees for weedy underbrush and overgrown fields.

Trim, compact, plain grayish-olive bird with wing bars,
eye stripe, and bright crown, orange in male and yellow in
female, bordered with black. Constantly active, flitting the
wings and hopping rapidly from branch to branch. Feeds
in any position. Call during migration is a thin, reedy, high-
pitched *see-see-see*. Song (rarely heard here) begins with hiss-
ing high notes and ends in a harsh descending chatter.

The slightly larger Ruby-crowned Kinglet, *R. calendula*, is
distinguished by its pronounced eye-ring, lack of head strip-
ing, and in the male a usually concealed red crown. It is a
common migrant in spring and fall, favoring low streamside
thickets and tangles, lingering rarely into December. Most
Ruby-crowns winter from Virginia south to Central America.
Call during migration, particularly when disturbed, consists
of a brief series of chattering, wrenlike notes. Its song is a
lilting, musical, descending warble, surprisingly loud for so
small a bird.

The food of kinglets is largely insects, their eggs and larvae.

CEDAR WAXWING, *Bombycilla cedrorum*

Slightly larger than a House Sparrow. Widely distributed,
irregular permanent resident, more common in migration
(especially May and October); nesting in our less urban
counties, more frequently on the mainland than on Long
Island. May be found in a variety of places — city parks,
suburban gardens, open woodlands, deciduous and coniferous
groves — but never in deep woods. Except in the nesting
season, Cedar Waxwings roam the countryside in small flocks.

Adult bird, either sex, has a satiny plumage, brown above
and yellow below, an alert crest, tail tipped broadly with
yellow, and wings sometimes with waxy red "tabs." Juvenile
is duller, faintly streaked below, with a smaller crest. Though
songless, Cedar Waxwings are quietly vociferous in any
season, giving peculiarly high-pitched wheezes and lisping
notes that always reveal their presence.

Nest placed on branch of a tree (deciduous or coniferous),
or in crotch of a bush or hedge, usually 5 to 20 feet from
ground; made by both sexes, of bark, twigs, grasses, and
rootlets to form a deep cup lined with soft material. Eggs: 4
to 5, pale bluish gray, lightly dotted with brown or black.
Incubation: 12 days, probably by female only. Both parents
feed the young, which remain in the nest about 16 days.

Waxwings are especially fond of cherries and other small
fruits, but also take much animal food — beetles, caterpillars,
and other insects. They often pursue insects, snapping them
up on the wing, flycatcher fashion.

STARLING, *Sturnus vulgaris*

Smaller than a Robin. First successfully introduced to North America at Central Park in 1890, and now a permanent and abundant resident, being uncommon only in the wildest woodlands remaining in our northern counties. After the nesting season, scattered families join into flocks that converge on favored roosting grounds nightly by the thousands, huddling close together for warmth. A roost estimated at 80,000 uses the understructure of the railroad viaduct in Manhattan at West 125th Street. Many suburban communities have bothersome Starling congregations.

Adults are chunky "blackbirds," with glossy black plumage and bright yellow bill. In the fall and winter, the plumage is conspicuously speckled and the bill dusky. Juveniles are uniformly grayish brown. Starlings can be distinguished from true blackbirds by their heavier appearance, short tail and direct (never undulating) rapid flight. Their calls are a variety of wheezes, chatters, and clear whistles. Some are excellent mimics of towhees, catbirds, cardinals, and jays.

Nests placed in most any kind of hole or cavity such as in a tree, old building, fence post, or birdhouse; made by both sexes, of grasses, twigs, and stems, and lined with finer materials. Eggs: 4 or 5, bluish white. Incubation: 12 to 13 days, by both sexes. Both parents feed the young, which stay in the nest 20 to 22 days. Two broods raised per year.

Omnivorous, eating many insects, berries and other wild fruits, and grains. Will come to bird feeders for suet.

RED-EYED VIREO, *Vireo olivaceus*

The size of a House Sparrow. Summer resident, widely distributed wherever there are mature deciduous woodlands; also frequently found in shade trees of suburbia. Arrives in early May and departs in early October.

Both sexes alike and inconspicuously colored, white below and olive above, with a white eye stripe and a blue-gray cap; no wing bars. The red color of the eye is seldom noticeable. Juveniles similar. All day long throughout the first half of summer one may hear the Red-eyed Vireo's pleasant but monotonous song — short warbled phrases, some rising and others falling in pitch like a question followed by an answer, about one per second. The alarm note is a husky, down-slurred *queee*.

Nest hung from a fork of a tree limb, usually 5 to 30 feet from the ground; made by female of birchbark, wasp paper, cottony materials, and bark fibers, woven into a deep cup and lined with finer fibers and pine needles. Eggs: 3 or 4, white, sparsely dotted with reddish brown. Incubation: 12 to 14 days, by female. Incubating birds can sometimes be touched without causing them to leave the nest. Both parents feed the young, which remain in the nest for 11 to 12 days.

Food largely insects, many of which are caterpillars, but some wild fruits are taken. Vireos feed inconspicuously near the treetops, but soon announce their presence with song. Compared with warblers, their movements are deliberate and unhurried.

BLACK-AND-WHITE WARBLER, *Mniotilta varia*

Smaller than a House Sparrow. One of our earliest and most abundant migrant warblers, less common as a summer resident (late April to October) in the more wooded areas, particularly the northern half of Long Island, Westchester, and the northern counties. Prefers open parks and woodlands, but during "waves" found in most any place with trees.

Identified by black and white streaked pattern all over, black throat and cheek patch, and striped head. Female like male but scarcely streaked below. (The only other common warbler predominantly black and white is the male Blackpoll Warbler, *Dendroica striata*, which has a white cheek and black cap.) Usually seen climbing about tree trunks or limbs, up, down, around, like a nuthatch. The song is a thin, wiry *weesee-weesee-weesee-weesee-weesee.* Another song sometimes heard is *weesee-weesee-weesee-weesee-woosee-woosee-weesee,* the *woosee* notes lower-pitched.

Nest placed on the ground, often protected by a log, stump, or sapling; made of leaves, mosses, fine fibers, and grasses and lined with fine roots and grasses. Eggs: 4 to 5, white, spotted or blotched with reddish brown. Incubation: 13 days. Both parents feed the nestlings.

The food consists of many kinds of bark insects, including eggs and pupae, ants, beetles, moths, and caterpillars; also spiders and daddy long-legs. The Blackpoll Warbler forages for insects in the foliage rather than on the trunks and limbs of trees.

PARULA WARBLER, *Parula americana*

Our smallest warbler (4½ inches long) and one of the most abundant warblers during migration, from late April into early June, and late August to mid-October. It is often in the company of other warblers and is always abundant during the warbler waves in May and September. It passes the winter mainly in the southern parts of Florida, Mexico, and Central America. Formerly nested in eastern and northern Long Island wherever there was *Usnea* lichen ("graybeard moss"), but with the disappearance of this plant in which it nested, it probably no longer breeds there.

Adult male in spring, gray-blue above (with greenish-

yellow patch on upper back) and two white wing bars. Yellow below, with dark red band across breast and white belly. Female in spring and adults in fall are similar, but less brightly marked and lack the dark red chestband.

The Parula Warbler stays up near the tops of trees, where it darts and flutters about after insects. During spring migration it favors the emerging "blossoms" of oaks and other deciduous trees, now disappearing in the quaking foliage, now shooting across open space to another tree. It is a persistent singer, the song being a buzzy, rapidly ascending trill or sizzle, ending with a loud, final *zip,* thus: *zree-ee-ee-zip.* The song is sometimes introduced as a series of *zree-zree-zree* notes.

The Parula Warbler is, like other members of its family, almost entirely insectivorous, taking many larvae that feed on foliage.

YELLOW WARBLER, *Dendroica petechia*

Much smaller than a House Sparrow. Our most abundant summer-resident warbler, found in brushy country with scattered trees, in willows beside water, in shrubbery or parks, and in hedges around gardens. Arrives late in April and departs in September.

Both sexes are bright yellow all over, the male with reddish streaks on breast and sides. In fall, both sexes appear somewhat duller. The song is a cheery, emphatic *tsee-tsee-tsee-tsee-titiwee,* accented on the last note.

The cuplike nest is built by both sexes in the fork of a bush or small tree, 3 to 8 feet from the ground; made of cottony materials, fine grasses, and rootlets; lined with feathers, long hairs, and plant down. Eggs: 3 to 5, variable, but mostly grayish or greenish white with a wreath of brownish black spots. Incubation: 11 days, by female. Both parents feed the young, which leave the nest in 9 to 12 days.

The Brown-headed Cowbird often lays eggs in the Yellow Warbler's nest. The host then deserts the nest or builds another nest floor over the Cowbird's egg. Nests with 6 Cowbird eggs, separated by as many nest bottoms, have been found.

Food, gleaned from the leaves and twigs of trees and shrubs, consists almost entirely of spiders and a wide variety of small insects, both adults and larvae. The Yellow Warbler is an attractive, useful bird to have in the garden.

MYRTLE WARBLER, *Dendroica coronata*

Smaller than a House Sparrow. Abundant spring and fall migrant, probably the warbler seen most often by bird watchers during the average year. During migration (mid-

April to late May, and mid-September onward), may be found almost anywhere: city parks, suburban gardens, woodlands, rural areas, and beaches. Often they outnumber all other warblers combined. In some years they winter in large numbers, especially along the south shore of Long Island.

All Myrtle Warblers, regardless of sex, age, or the season, have a yellow rump, conspicuous in flight. Spring males have bluish back, white underparts with black on breast and sides, and yellow crown and side patches. Spring females are similar but have more brown above, while adults and immatures in fall are distinctly brownish and streaked below. Song is a listless trill, variable in pitch; call a loud, easily recognizable *check*. The only other warblers with yellow rumps are the Magnolia, *D. magnolia,* and the Cape May, *D. tigrina.* Both are yellow below, whereas the Myrtle is not.

Food of Myrtle Warblers in warmer months consists of insects and their larvae and spiders. In searching for insects, Myrtles cover trees from ground to top, investigating twigs and leaves and probing into crevices of bark. Often they dart after insects like flycatchers. In winter, Myrtles depend largely on wild fruits. Thus it is commonplace to see flocks of Myrtles gathering them on the bayberry, poison ivy, and red cedar that grow back from the beaches and on the moorlands. Sometimes Myrtles visit feeders for doughnuts and suet.

BLACKPOLL WARBLER, *Dendroica striata*

Smaller than a House Sparrow. Common late spring and fall migrant. Probably the most abundant warbler during the last third of May and early June. Reappears in mid-September and migrates through the New York City area until mid-October. Found in woodlands and parks, where it frequents the tops of trees, but at the height of spring migration it even appears in trees and shrubs along streets and in suburban gardens.

Adult male in spring has a black cap, white face, olive back streaked with black, two white wing bars, underparts white, with black streaks running from corner of bill down along sides of body. Female in spring is paler in appearance with no black cap and white face. Both adults in fall and immatures are entirely different in appearance, with back brighter green, streaks fainter, and underparts distinctly yellowish. The song is a thin, wiry, high-pitched *zi-zi-zi-zi-zi* repeated as many as 15 times, increasing and then decreasing in volume. It may be given slowly or rapidly.

Blackpoll Warblers breed in the coniferous forests of the Catskills and Adirondacks of Upstate New York and elsewhere farther north. On passing southward through our area in the fall, they are bound for southern Florida, whence they take off over the Caribbean for their wintering grounds in northern South America. They return by the same route.

The food consists of small spiders and many minute insects gathered from tree foliage.

OVENBIRD, *Seiurus aurocapillus*

The size of House Sparrow. Summer resident, found commonly in deep woodlands of outlying counties where trees are high and undergrowth thin. Still nests in some of the less disturbed city parks. Arrives late in April and departs in mid-October.

Both sexes alike, olive-brown above, with orange and black crown stripes, and white below, streaked with black. More often heard than seen. The Ovenbird announces its presence with a ringing song, *teacher-teacher-teacher-teacher-teacher-tea*, each note louder than the one before. Its singing perch is generally a low branch. Less familiar is its more musical flight song, to be heard most often at dusk or on moonlit nights. The Ovenbird spends much time on the forest floor, where it walks with a comical wag of its tail. When flushed, it will fly up a short distance to peer at the intruder, sometimes walking along the branch.

Nest is placed on the ground; made by the female of dried leaves, mosses, and twigs, and completely roofed over, with the entrance on the side like an oven (hence the bird's name). Eggs: 4 or 5, white, speckled with brown and gray. Incubation: 12 days, by female. Young remain in nest 8 days and are fed by both parents.

Food is mostly insects, spiders, snails, slugs, and earthworms.

YELLOWTHROAT, *Geothlypis trichas*

Smaller than a House Sparrow. Common summer resident. Found in brushy fields and roadsides, the brushy borders of streams and marshes, and parks that have thickets and tangles. Arrives about May 1 and remains until mid-October, with stragglers staying into December. In fall migration, it frequently appears in such places as gardens, orchards, and woodlands, where it rarely nests. It can often be lured from a brushy thicket by "squeaking."

Adult male has prominent black mask, olive-green above, bright yellow on the throat and breast, becoming white on the belly. Adult female and juveniles lack the black mask. The usual song is a loud, clear *witchity-witchity-witchity*, occasionally ending with an added note, *witch*. Less frequently observed is the flight song, consisting of a long series of chips, with *witchity* sounds sometimes interjected, and given while the bird is from 6 to 20 feet in the air. The Yellowthroat's call is a harsh, unmistakable *tschact*.

Nest placed on the ground or in a bush or dense clump of

vegetation, usually well concealed; made of grasses, plant stems, and leaves, deeply cupped and bulky and lined with soft materials but no down. Eggs: usually 4, white, speckled with brown. Incubation: 12 days, by female. Both parents feed the young, which stay in nest about 10 days.

Food consists almost entirely of insects.

AMERICAN REDSTART, *Setophaga ruticilla*

Smaller than a House Sparrow. Fairly common summer resident in second-growth deciduous woodlands, arriving in early May and departing late in October. One of the commonest migrant warblers with peak numbers in mid-May and mid-September; found during migration in almost any leafy habitat from Central Park to the woodlands of the outlying counties.

A bird of seemingly perpetual animation. If it is not flitting from one limb to another, it is hopping along a limb, its wings drooping and tail fanned out, or darting out to snap up an insect in the air. Adult male mostly black, with white below and orange-red on the wings and sides of body and tail. Adult female similarly patterned but with olive-gray in place of black, and yellow in place of orange-red. Juveniles and first-year males are like adult females. Several different songs, a common one being a sibilant *see-see-see-see-swee.*

Nest usually built in the crotch of a deciduous sapling, 5 to 30 feet (average 7 feet) from the ground; made by female, compactly formed of fine strips of bark and rootlets, held together by spider webbing, sometimes covered with lichens and bits of birchbark, and lined with soft material such as hair. Eggs: usually 4; whitish, delicately spotted with brown toward larger end. Incubation: 12 days, by female. Both parents feed the young, which stay in nest 8 days.

Strictly insectivorous, gleaning eggs, larvae, and adults from trees, and capturing insects on the wing, flycatcher style.

HOUSE SPARROW, *Passer domesticus*

Also called English Sparrow. Length 6⅓ inches. Not a sparrow at all but a weaver finch, introduced into New York City from Europe in 1850 and now found continent-wide. One of our most familiar and adaptable birds, found everywhere from the smallest Manhattan park to rural roadsides in outlying counties. Usually found in flocks except when nesting. Aggressive, it will often usurp the nesting sites of native species and in winter monopolize feeding trays.

Adult male has black throat (veiled in winter), gray crown, and white cheeks, a conspicuous white wing bar, and grayish-white underparts. Adult female and juveniles grayish brown without black throat and other prominent markings. Vocal sounds comprise a loud *cheeep,* frequently repeated, and numerous twitterings.

Nests placed commonly in cavities, as in a tree, building, or birdhouse, but lodged sometimes openly in branches of thickly foliaged trees, 10 to 50 feet from the ground. Nesting materials are grasses, straw, twigs, feathers, rags, twine, bits of paper, etc. A nest in a cavity is a structureless mass of these materials filling the entire space, except for a pocket to contain the eggs, while a nest in the open is a bulky, globular structure, largely of grasses, straw, and twigs with an entrance at one side. Incubation: 12 days, by female. Both parents feed the young which stay in nest for 17 days. Several broods annually.

Omnivorous, eating a wide variety of plant and animal matter.

EASTERN MEADOWLARK, *Sturnella magna*

The size of a Robin, but chunkier, with large feet and short tail. Summer resident in the more open country: upland fields, meadows, cultivated farms, golf courses — wherever deep grass may be found. Common but decreasing as habitat disappears. Meadowlarks are among the first birds to appear in the spring, arriving in early March. Most leave by mid-November, but a few stay throughout the winter.

Adults yellow below, with a prominent black V on the breast; darkly streaked on the sides and variously barred and spotted above with brown, black, and buffy white. Adults and immatures in fall and winter browner and the black V veiled with buffy. Meadowlarks can be recognized in flight by their white outer tail feathers, which show plainly, and by their wing action, which alternates between rapid beating and sailing. The Eastern Meadowlark's song is a slowly and clearly whistled *say-you, see-here.* Alarm call is a loud chatter.

Nest placed on the ground, in a slight depression, usually concealed by dense grasses; made of grasses, some of which are pulled over the top, forming a dome with an entrance at one side. Eggs: 4 to 6, white, spotted with reddish brown. Incubation: 13 to 14 days, by female. Both parents feed the young, which stay in nest 11 or 12 days.

Food consists commonly of insects, when they are available, seeds and grains at other times.

RED-WINGED BLACKBIRD, *Agelaius phoeniceus*

Smaller than a Robin. Abundant summer resident from early March to mid-November in a wide variety of habitats, but prefers meadows, marshes, and other wetlands supporting sedges, cattails, bulrushes, etc. Outstandingly adaptable, now nests in fields and bushes and along weedy roadsides. In late

summer and fall may be seen at dusk moving in large flocks
to nocturnal roosts. Winters in small numbers in sheltered
places, coming regularly to feeders.

Adult male entirely black except for scarlet wing patches
margined behind with buffy white. Female heavily streaked
brown and buffy above, black and grayish white below.
Juveniles similar to the female, but buffier above and faintly
pinkish below. The Red-wing's song is a liquid gurgling
o-kur-glee, given as it fluffs out its feathers and spreads its wings
to display scarlet patches. Its most common notes are a husky
chack and a high-pitched whistled *tee-ah,* which is slurred
downward.

Nest usually suspended from among cattails, bulrushes,
etc., or lodged in bushes, a foot or more above water, but
sometimes on the ground in sedges or grasses; made of cattail
leaves, sedge blades, and coarse grasses woven into a deep cup
and lined with finer plant material. Eggs: 3 to 5, bluish white,
variously spotted and lined with black and purple. Incubation: 11 days, by female. Both parents feed the young, which
stay in nest 10 or 11 days.

Food consists largely of insects during the nesting season, of
plant matter (weed seeds, small fruits, and grains) in other
seasons.

BALTIMORE ORIOLE, *Icterus galbula*

Smaller than a Robin. Summer resident in suburban and
more rural areas, preferring shade trees in towns and to a less
extent the woodlands bordering fields, lakes, and streams.
Absent in dense woodlands. Arrives early in May and departs
in September.

Adult male bright orange and black; single white wing bar.
Adult female and juveniles duller, with orange replaced by
yellow, black by olive-brown; two wing bars. The song is a
short, disconnected series of loud, flutelike notes, scarcely suggesting a complete song. There is much variation. Call is a
two-syllabled whistle, *tew-lee;* alarm note is a loud chatter.

Nest usually suspended from the end of a long swaying
branch, but occasionally from branches near the top of a tree,
15 to 60 feet from the ground; made of long plant fibers, strips
of bark, string, and similarly pliable materials, intricately
woven into a deep pouch and lined with hair and fine grasses.
Eggs: 4 to 6, white, blotched and scrawled with black and
brown. Incubation: 12 to 14 days, by female. Both parents
feed the young, which stay in nest about 2 weeks. Two or
three days before leaving, the young begin calling loudly and
incessantly.

About 80 per cent of the food is animal matter, consisting
of many caterpillars and other insects. Small fruits and weed
seeds make up most of the plant matter.

COMMON GRACKLE, *Quiscalus quiscula*

Also called Purple Grackle and Bronzed Grackle. Larger than a Robin. Widespread summer resident in open country and all but the densest urban areas. Often appearing on suburban lawns and frequenting parks. Prefers the vicinity of thickly foliaged shade trees and large conifers, also the densely wooded borders of streams and wet places where it roosts. Arrives in early March, departs in late November, but a few remain into January. Grackles are notably gregarious, usually nesting in colonies, gathering in communal roosts, and migrating in large flocks.

Black birds with yellow eyes and long wedge-shaped tail that is troughed. Male brilliant iridescent blue (especially on head), violet, and bronze; female somewhat smaller and duller. Juveniles dull brownish black throughout. Vocal sounds include a hoarse *chack* and a song made up of a series of creaky, sometimes gurgling or liquid notes, terminating in a rasping squawk.

Nest — a bulky, cupped structure of grasses, weed stems, and twigs, strengthened with mud and lined with grasses — is often high in a dense conifer, but may be in other thick growth, in a tree cavity, or under a bridge. Eggs: 3 to 5, bluish, boldly spotted and scrawled with black and brown. Incubation: 14 days, by female. Both parents feed the young.

Food includes many ground-inhabiting insects together with seeds, nuts, small fruits, and waste grain.

BROWN-HEADED COWBIRD, *Molothrus ater*

Smaller than a Robin. Widespread summer resident except in dense woodlands and the densest urban areas. Common in parks, suburban gardens, and open country. When there are cattle it frequently follows them, catching insects stirred up by their feet. Cowbirds arrive early in mid-March and depart by mid-November. Many stay through the winter, foraging in small flocks. During migration, they often flock with other blackbirds.

Adult male with coffee-brown head and neck; rest of plumage glossy black with greenish reflections. Female smaller, grayish brown. Juveniles similar to female but buffier and noticeably streaked. The commonest song is composed of two gurgly notes, *bub-klo*, followed by a higher-pitched, sibilant *seek-kt-seek*. Call notes include a *see-purr*, the first part higher than the second, and a *chuck*.

The Cowbird is a social parasite, laying its eggs in the nests of other species that are usually smaller and build open nests. Eggs: whitish, uniformly speckled with gray and brown. As many as 25 eggs may be laid by one Cowbird in a season, but rarely more than one egg in a nest. Two or more Cowbird eggs in a nest are usually laid by different females. Incubation period: 11 to 12 days, by host species. Young birds are reared by the host species only and stay in nest 10 to 11 days.

Many insects are eaten by Cowbirds, but their food is chiefly plant material.

SCARLET TANAGER, *Piranga olivacea*

Larger than a House Sparrow. Regular summer resident, preferring open deciduous woodlands and open parklands with shade trees. Arrives in early May and departs by mid-October. More common in migration, especially in fall in woodlands on the outer beach strip.

Male bright red, with black wings and tail; female and juveniles olive-green above and yellowish below (streaked in juveniles). Male in winter like female but still retains black wings and tail. When changing into winter plumage during late summer, male appears blotchy, owing to patches of new body feathers replacing old red ones. Song suggests a Robin's but is slower and has a buzzy quality. Call is a distinctly uttered *chip-perr.*

Nest placed far out on limb of a tree, usually deciduous, 10 to 40 feet from the ground; loosely made of rootlets, pine needles, twigs, grasses, and pieces of bark, forming a thin-walled shallow cup, sparsely lined with grasses, in which eggs may be seen from below. Eggs: 3 or 4, pale greenish, speckled at large end with reddish brown. Incubation: 13 to 14 days, by female. Both parents feed the young.

Primarily insectivorous. The Scarlet Tanager depends mainly on insects that infest foliage, consequently gathers most of its food high in trees, but now and then it resorts to foraging on the ground, occasionally on lawns. It will sometimes feed on berries of various kinds, especially mulberries.

CARDINAL, *Richmondena cardinalis*

Smaller than a Robin. Permanent resident, increasing everywhere, least common (except for urban counties) on Long Island. Prefers areas with shrubby thickets, such as woodland edges, garden borders, roadsides, parks, and cemeteries.

Both sexes have a high crest and red bill. Male red, brightest on breast, with black between bill and eye and on throat; female and juveniles grayish brown above, grayish buff below, with a rosy tinge to crest, wings, and tail. Song is a loud, pleasantly whistled series of phrases, *what-year, what-year, whit-whit-whit,* or simply *whit-whit-whit* or *whirly-whirly-whirly.* Call is a short distinctive *tink.*

Nest placed in a thickly foliaged shrub, vine, or conifer, 4 to 8 feet from the ground; a thin, deep cup, rather loosely made by female, of grasses, twigs, and weed stems and scantily lined with rootlets and other fine materials. Eggs: 3 or 4, greenish white, speckled with reddish brown and gray. Incubation: 12 to 13 days, by female. Both parents feed the young, which stay in nest 9 to 10 days. Usually two, sometimes three, broods a year.

Although a variety of insects are consumed by Cardinals, their principal food consists of wild fruits and seeds. Feeding shelves are attractive to Cardinals as long as they are well supplied with sunflower seeds.

ROSE-BREASTED GROSBEAK,
Pheucticus ludovicianus

Smaller than Robin; bill stout and conical. Common migrant from late April to late May and mid-September to late October. Partial in the spring to the pale emerging foliage of all tall oaks. Less common but widespread summer resident in the suburban and more rural counties, where it prefers open second-growth deciduous woodlands adjoining areas of tall shrubby growth, and also orchards and shade trees about farms, estates, or in towns and parks where there is abundant shrubbery.

Adult male black and white, with a rose-red triangular patch on the breast; bill white. Female and juveniles brownish and sparrow-like in appearance, being striped below; two whitish wing bars; bill dark. The song is like a Robin's, but sweeter, more melodious, and rapid. The call most often heard is a sharp *kick,* metallic and distinctive.

Nest placed in a tree or high shrub, 5 to 25 feet from the ground; loosely made of twigs, stems, and rootlets, forming a cup so thin that the eggs show through from below; practically no lining. Eggs: 3 to 5, pale blue-green with brownish spots. Incubation: 12 to 13 days, by both sexes (the male occasionally sings while incubating). Both parents feed the young, which stay in nest 10 or more days.

About half the food consists of insects and other animal matter, the rest seeds and wild fruits.

AMERICAN GOLDFINCH, *Spinus tristis*

Erroneously called Wild Canary. Smaller than a House Sparrow. Widespread permanent resident, breeding in mid-summer (later than most other birds) and present in every month of the year, but most abundant during migrations from mid-April to mid-May and in September and October. Except in the breeding season, notably gregarious, occurring in small flocks everywhere but in the deepest woodlands and dense urban districts. Prefers parklands, suburbia, and the edges of woodlands near weedy fields.

Male lemon-yellow, with black forecrown, wings, and tail; two wing bars, one white and one buffy; inner webs of tail feathers white. Female yellow-brown above, dull yellow below; no crown patch; wings and tail not so black and contrastingly marked. Male and immatures in fall and winter resemble female. The Goldfinch has two songs. One is canary-like, being a long series of spirited, musical twitters, but lacks the melodious trills of the cage-bird. The other song, given on the wing, is *per-chick-o-ree,* repeated each time the bird bounds upward during its deeply undulating flight. The usual call is an inquiring *chee-eep,* with a rising inflection.

Nest placed in a thickly foliaged shrub or tree, 3 to 30 feet from the ground; compactly made of fine grasses and cottony materials, forming a thick-walled cup, and lined with thistle-down. Eggs: 3 to 6, pale blue. Incubation: 12 days, by female. Both parents feed the young, which stay in nest about 13 days.

Small seeds, such as those of thistles, dandelions, and rag-weed, constitute most of the food, although insects and wild fruits are occasionally included.

RUFOUS-SIDED TOWHEE, *Pipilo erythrophthalmus*

Slightly smaller than a Robin. Abundant migrant from early April to mid-May and mid-September to late October. Widespread common summer resident, preferring dry, brushy country, parks, overgrown gardens, and open woodlands, particularly the pine-oak scrub of eastern Long Island. Winters in small numbers where there are sheltered areas.

Male black, with sides reddish brown and belly white; wings and tail show white during flight; eyes bright red. Female similarly patterned but with black replaced by grayish brown. Juveniles very sparrow-like, being reddish brown above, yellowish below, and streaked. The song, almost invariably given from the top of a bush or tree, is distinctive and resembles *drink your teeeee,* the first syllable being loud and sharp, the last trilled. No less distinctive is the call — a loud, often repeated *to-whee,* or *che-wink* — usually heard from the underbrush. There is also a metallic *chink.*

Nest usually placed on the ground under a shrub or clump of ferns, but occasionally in a low bush or tangle; made of grasses, leaves, bark, and rootlets, forming a cup, and lined with fine materials. Eggs: 4 or 5, white, finely speckled, sometimes blotched, with reddish brown. Incubation: 12 to 13 days, by female. Both parents feed the young.

Food consists of insects, seeds, and wild fruits. Most of this material the Towhee obtains on the ground by scratching noisily among the leaves.

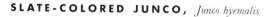

SLATE-COLORED JUNCO, *Junco hyemalis*

The size of a House Sparrow. Common migrant in both spring and fall; common — in some years abundant — winter visitor. Found almost anywhere, from suburban gardens to the larger city parks. Usually in small flocks. Preferred habitat is open country adjacent to coniferous groves or mixed woodlands.

Adult males slaty gray, sometimes slightly brownish on wings and back, with white belly sharply defined against dark gray breast; outer tail feathers white, showing plainly in flight; bill pink. Adult female similar but duller and browner. Juveniles sparrow-like, being brown and conspicuously streaked above and below. The song is a rapid series of 8 to 20 or more simple notes on the same pitch, much like a Chipping Sparrow's but more musical; alarm note is *tsick,* usually given in a series.

The Junco breeds just north of our area in the higher altitudes of the Catskill Mountains. Nest placed on the ground, in a depression, frequently in a mossy bank or under something such as the roots of a stump; made of grasses, rootlets, and mosses, forming a deep cup, and lined with fine materials. Eggs: usually 4, white, spotted with brown. Incubation: 11 to 12 days. Both parents feed the young, which stay in nest 12 days.

About 20 per cent of the Junco's food consists of insects and spiders, the rest vegetal matter — mostly weed seeds and occasional small wild fruits.

TREE SPARROW, *Spizella arborea*

Approximately the length of a House Sparrow, but more slender. Widespread winter visitor in the less urban sections, often abundant in some winters and scarce in others. Frequents weedy fields, hedges, brushy woodland borders, and frozen-over marshes. Tree Sparrows usually appear in early October and may remain well into April. They nest in the North Country where the spruce forests meet the arctic tundra.

Adults predominantly brownish gray and streaked above, with a reddish-brown crown and two white wing bars; grayish white and unstreaked below, with a prominent dark spot in the center of the breast. The Chipping and Field Sparrows, *S. passerina* and *S. pusilla,* are similar in appearance, but lack the dark breast spot. Toward spring an occasional Tree Sparrow may be heard giving its song — canary-like notes, the first long, clear, and high-pitched, the others rapidly uttered in a musical trill.

Tree Sparrows are usually seen in small flocks. A common sight after a snowfall is a flock dropping down to a weed patch in search of seeds. Some members of the flock immediately begin picking up seeds that have fallen on the snow, while others obtain more by hopping on the weeds and opening the seed pods. As wintering Tree Sparrows are almost entirely dependent on seeds, they are often attracted to feeding stations that are liberally and regularly supplied with small grains.

CHIPPING SPARROW, *Spizella passerina*

Smaller and more slender than a House Sparrow. Common but decreasing summer resident in suburban and rural areas; very common in migration from early April to mid-May and in September, with a few lingering into December. Found frequently about houses, along roadsides, in parks and cemeteries, and on golf courses.

Adults have a reddish-brown cap and a black line through the eye and a whitish line over it; underparts grayish white; bill black. Juveniles lack the distinctive head markings and are noticeably streaked below. The song is an unmusical trill of about 15 to 30 notes on the same pitch. The alarm note is *tsip*.

Birds similar to Chipping Sparrow: Field Sparrow, *S. pusilla*, found in shrubby fields, lacks distinctive cap, and has pink bill. The Tree Sparrow (see preceding account), absent in summer, and Swamp Sparrow, *Melospiza georgiana*, found in marshes, have reddish caps, but former has prominent spot on breast and latter has reddish brown on wings and back.

Nest of the Chipping Sparrow is placed in a bush, vine, or tree, usually 3 to 6 feet, but sometimes up to 20 feet, from the ground; made of grasses and rootlets, forming a neat cup, and lined with fine materials including long hairs. Eggs: 3 to 5, pale blue, wreathed at the larger end with dark spots. Incubation: 11 to 12 days. Both parents feed the young, which remain in nest about 12 days.

Chipping Sparrows feed on the ground, picking up many caterpillars and other insects during the summer, mostly small seeds in other seasons.

WHITE-THROATED SPARROW,
Zonotrichia albicollis

Slightly larger than a House Sparrow. Abundant migrant in spring and fall and common winter visitant. Found almost anywhere from open woodlands to suburban gardens, brushy fields, parks, and marshes. Arrives early in September and departs by mid-May. Breeds in the higher elevations of our northern counties. During migrations in the spring and fall White-throats move in flocks, often stopping to scratch in the leaves under dooryard shrubbery.

Adults have a white throat contrasting sharply with gray breast; yellow between bill and eye. Like the less common White-crowned Sparrow (*Z. leucophrys*), they have black and white crown stripes, but White-crowns lack the white throat and yellow spot and have a pink bill. Juvenile White-throats are generally duskier than the adults, with less distinct markings and a streaked breast. The song of the White-throat is a high-pitched, clear, whistled *oh-teee-whey, whey, whey;* alarm note is a loud, metallic *tink*. The call generally given during migration is a faint, lisping *sst*.

Nest placed on the ground (sometimes sunk in a hummock) near or under a bush or pile of brush; made by female, of grasses, mosses, and rootlets with fine materials such as hair or feathers for lining. Eggs: 4 or 5, pale greenish or bluish, spotted with reddish brown toward larger end. Incubation: 12 to 14 days, by female.

Feeds on the ground, chiefly by scratching. Food consists of insects such as beetles and grasshoppers, also spiders, weed seeds, and berries.

SONG SPARROW, *Melospiza melodia*

The size of a House Sparrow. Common, widespread permanent resident, except in the most urban areas. Numbers are highest during spring and fall migrations, lowest in winter. Found wherever there is brushy country or shrubbery, in gardens, parks, roadsides, and meadows and on the edges of streams and marshes.

Adults reddish brown above, streaked with gray and black; white below, heavily streaked with black; a dark blotch in the middle of the breast. Juveniles similar but buffier. The song is a variable series of musical sounds, usually beginning with three clear notes of identical pitch and quality, followed by one or more trills of varying pitch. Call note is a loud *tshink*.

Birds similar to Song Sparrow: Savannah Sparrow, *Passerculus sandwichensis,* common summer resident of meadows and grassy dunes; slightly forked tail and pale yellow before eye. Vesper Sparrow, *Pooecetes gramineus,* uncommon summer resident of upland fields; reddish brown at bend of wing and white outer tail feathers.

Song Sparrow nest is placed on the ground in a sheltered situation, or more rarely in a low bush or conifer; made of grasses, rootlets, etc., lined with finer materials. Eggs: 3 to 5, greenish, speckled with brown. Incubation: 12 to 14 days, by female. Both parents feed the young, which remain in nest 9 to 10 days.

About one-third of the food is animal matter, chiefly insects; the rest is seeds and other vegetal material. Practically all food is obtained on the ground.

WHERE TO FIND BIRDS
AROUND NEW YORK CITY

A VISITOR approaching New York City by air, with a desire to see some of the birds of the region, would find his first glimpse of our metropolis disheartening. Below him is what appears to be one unbroken, monotonous sweep of urban development crowding every waterway, covering every acre, reaching every hilltop. The same scene at night, although beautiful, is even less encouraging. The entire world is ablaze with lights, and lights mean people, and people mean few birds.

The truth is quite the contrary: few large cities in the world are so well endowed by nature and by man for enjoyable indulgence in this most delightful of avocations, the study of birds. Concealed down there in the urban sprawl are a host of places where the wild bird still may be watched, heard, and studied. Parks, marshes, forests, harbors, beaches, bays, backyards — yes even garbage dumps and sewer outlets. Nowhere in the city is one more than a mile from a leafy square, a waterfront, a patch of shrubbery that affords an opportunity to observe birds.

New York City and its nearby counties have produced records for more than 400 species, and almost every year the list creeps upward. This increment of unexpected birds keeps even the most blasé of oldtimers alert and eager. Who knows but what you might discover a species completely new to the region, this very morning?

There are many reasons for this felicitous state of affairs. Having a climate with a wide range of moods, New York can be arctic tundra with subzero winds and a Texas valley with 100-degree heat, all in the same year. It lies directly athwart the Atlantic flyway, and its shorelines, rivers, and ridges serve as flightlines for migrating birds. Few cities offer as thrilling a spectacle of the passage of hordes of migrant birds as sweep over in spring and fall. New York is water-rimmed, its eastern arm reaching far out into the Atlantic Ocean. That brings the constant concourse of pelagic birds, as well as waifs and strays from overseas. New York is a geographic discontinuity: the barrier beaches form in the fall a haven — the land's end — for thousands of migrants carried oceanward by prevailing off-continent winds. The result is an unusual concentration of "western" or "southwestern" vagrants. And again, New York is in the track of tropical hurricanes, bringing the possibility of strangers from southern seas. Lastly, New York stands in the Transition Zone — just between the Carolinian and the Hudsonian faunal types — giving us the most northern breeding sites for some southern species, and most southern sites for some northern species. In a single year, a bird watcher may see Boreal Chickadee and Glossy Ibis, Brown Pelican and Common Murre, Common (European) Teal and Scissor-tailed Flycatcher — as well as species that breed in Alaska, Yukon Territory, Ungava, Greenland, Florida, Oklahoma, the Antarctic, and perhaps even in Siberia. What is more, he may reach in three hours by car from Times Square the nesting areas of as many as 160 species.

Just what is the New York City of this book? Mindful that there will be other books in this series, we are confining our boundaries to the five city boroughs (Manhattan, Brooklyn, Queens, the Bronx, Richmond), the two eastern counties of Long Island (Nassau and Suffolk), and the adjacent up-state counties of Westchester, Putnam, Dutchess, Rockland, and Orange. Also included are three sites in New Jersey, one in Connecticut, and one in Ulster County, New York. See the endpapers map.

No place is much more than three hours from Times Square by car, and the variety of habitats is remarkable. Some are man-made, others man-altered; man has changed the topography and introduced new plants as well as the most conspicuous birds. Some places are almost primeval in their unspoiled beauty, and a few places in certain seasons give the illusion at least of being untouched by man.

Because of its great diversity, the New York region does not lend itself to simple habitat groupings. The climax forests, the remnants of true prairie that stretched eastward from Hempstead, and most of the freshwater marshes are almost gone, and everywhere distinctive habitats have merged into the artificial habitat of the city. Remembering this we shall attempt to describe what was once here and now remains only in fragments.

Long Island, south of the two moraine ridges that transect it from east to west, is a sandy outwash plain, flat, featureless, and originally covered either with open fields and meadows, or (in the poorest soils) the familiar oak-pine barrens, with their laurel ground cover. Parts of the plain that are almost pure sand will support red cedar, wild cherry, gray birch, and bayberry — often these areas run down to salt marsh. Along the richer margins of streams and in their shallow valleys a wide variety of deciduous trees abound, among them red maple, alder, willow, birch, and shadbush. North of the ridges the land is more rugged, with rolling hills and some rather steep-pitched valleys. The hills here are cloaked predominantly with oak and laurel, and the valleys forested with oak, maple, beech, tulip tree, and other hardwoods.

In New York City itself, these differences are maintained wherever the land has been left unchanged, but the far more prevalent habitat is the land-scaped park with its wide diversity of both native and exotic trees and shrubs. North of the city, the wooded areas, like northern Long Island, show a predominance of maple and beech, with birch, basswood, and white oak in evidence, while in the valleys oak, hickory, dogwood, laurel, and willow will be found. Throughout the region, suburban development means a mixture of the native and the imported; the streets lined with Norway or silver maple, sycamore, or American elm; the gardens graced with flowering trees and shrubs of a hundred different species.

BOBOLINK

Eastern Long Island is still primarily farmland, with fields of garden vegetables giving way in winter to rye. Along the southern shore of Long Island stretches the magnificent sand-barrier beach, with its dunes, its tidal flats, and its miles of phragmites and spartina.

To summarize, you will find woodland and parkland, evergreen groves, broad beaches, tidal estuaries, salt marshes, lakes and streams, meadows and moorland; habitats created by man that are no less inviting to birds: fields and farms, parks and cemeteries, orchards and estates, reservoirs with encircling pines; and to the satisfaction of every suburbanite, the thicket in the lot next door, the glade behind the garage, the feeder at the kitchen window. Each of these environments will attract in every season its own particular, ever-changing association of birds.

Before considering specific locations, it may be helpful to list below the major habitat types, with some of their most typical breeding species. See also page 130. An asterisk after the species means that it is local and uncommon. For more details on habitats and their bird species, you should consult such comprehensive books as *Birds around New York City* (1942) by Allan D. Cruickshank and *Birds of the New York Area* (1964) by John Bull.

AVERAGE LANDSCAPED AREAS, SUBURBIA, PARKS, ORCHARDS, WOODLAND EDGES (HABITAT A)

Sparrow Hawk	Barn Swallow	Yellow Warbler
Ring-necked Pheasant	Blue Jay	House Sparrow
Rock Dove (Pigeon)	Common Crow	Red-winged Blackbird
Mourning Dove	Black-capped Chickadee	Baltimore Oriole
Yellow-billed Cuckoo	Tufted Titmouse	Common Grackle
Black-billed Cuckoo	White-breasted Nuthatch	Brown-headed Cowbird
Screech Owl	House Wren	Cardinal
Chimney Swift	Catbird	House Finch
Ruby-throated Hummingbird	Brown Thrasher	American Goldfinch
	Robin	Rufous-sided Towhee
Yellow-shafted Flicker	Wood Thrush	Chipping Sparrow
Downy Woodpecker	Starling	Song Sparrow
Eastern Kingbird	Red-eyed Vireo	

BEACHES, DUNES (INCLUDING SHRUBBERY), THICKETS (HABITATS B, D)

Green Heron	Roseate Tern*	Yellow Warbler
Piping Plover	Least Tern	Yellowthroat
Spotted Sandpiper	Black Skimmer	Red-winged Blackbird
Great Black-backed Gull	(Prairie) Horned Lark	Rufous-sided Towhee
Herring Gull	Catbird	Savannah Sparrow
Common Tern	Brown Thrasher	Song Sparrow

AROUND OR NEAR FRESHWATER, INCLUDING MARSHES (HABITAT F)

Pied-billed Grebe	Wood Duck*	Barn Swallow
Green Heron	Marsh Hawk	Fish Crow* (coastal)
Black-crowned Night Heron	Virginia Rail	Long-billed Marsh Wren
American Bittern	Common Gallinule*	Yellow Warbler
Mute Swan	Spotted Sandpiper	Red-winged Blackbird
Canada Goose	Belted Kingfisher	Common Grackle
Mallard	Eastern Phoebe	Swamp Sparrow
Black Duck	Traill's Flycatcher*	Song Sparrow
	Rough-winged Swallow*	

WOODLAND, COPSES, GROVES, WOODED PARKS (HABITAT W)

Mourning Dove
Yellow-shafted Flicker
Hairy Woodpecker
Downy Woodpecker
Great Crested Flycatcher
Eastern Wood Pewee
Blue Jay
Common Crow
Black-capped Chickadee
Tufted Titmouse
  (rare Long Island)

White-breasted Nuthatch
Catbird
Brown Thrasher
Robin
Wood Thrush
Veery
Starling
Red-eyed Vireo
Black-and-white Warbler
Chestnut-sided Warbler
Ovenbird

American Redstart
Common Grackle
Brown-headed Cowbird
Scarlet Tanager
Rose-breasted Grosbeak
Rufous-sided Towhee
Song Sparrow

PINE-OAK SCRUB (HABITAT W)

Red-tailed Hawk*
Yellow-shafted Flicker
Downy Woodpecker
Blue Jay
Common Crow
Black-capped Chickadee

Hermit Thrush*
Prairie Warbler
Pine Warbler
Yellow Warbler
Yellowthroat

Catbird
Brown Thrasher
Field Sparrow
Chipping Sparrow
Song Sparrow

AROUND OR NEAR SALTWATER, INCLUDING SALT MARSHES
(HABITATS M, S)

Green Heron
American Bittern
Black Duck
Marsh Hawk
Clapper Rail

Long-billed Marsh Wren
Eastern Meadowlark
Red-winged Blackbird
Yellow Warbler
Yellowthroat

Sharp-tailed Sparrow
Seaside Sparrow
Swamp Sparrow
Savannah Sparrow
Song Sparrow

UPLANDS: FIELDS, MEADOWS, FARMS, GOLF COURSES,
OPEN COUNTRY ROADSIDES (HABITAT U)

Killdeer
Bobolink*
(Prairie) Horned Lark

Eastern Meadowlark
Grasshopper Sparrow
Vesper Sparrow

Field Sparrow
Song Sparrow

THE 200 LOCALITIES mentioned in the following pages are in three categories: one asterisk indicates locations primarily of interest to local residents; two asterisks indicate locations of greater interest or with one or two outstanding attractions; three asterisks indicate locations of widespread interest.

Naturally not all of the one-star locations have been included; every dedicated bird watcher has his own. We hope that we have included most of the two-star and all of the three-star locations. We emphasize that a regular systematic study of a site convenient to you can be more valuable than an infrequent excursion to a popular showplace.

All of the areas may be located on any good street map of New York City and the detailed maps of specific areas are indicated in the text. The directions, by car or public transportation, are from Manhattan, the preceding locality, or the nearest major highway, parkway, or turnpike (numbered whenever possible). A good road map is essential.

MANHATTAN: Our most urban county offers two basic habitats — parks and waterfronts. For much of the year, the parks are sadly bereft of bird life save for the Rock Dove, Starling, and House Sparrow. The summer-resident list is more generous, and during the spring and fall migrations the parks, squares, churchyards, even the smallest green plots, come alive with birds. Manhattan can be a haven for migrating birds; it can also be a menace, for on certain foggy nights in autumn, when a sudden lowering of the ceiling and following winds combine, our tallest buildings take a toll of landbirds by the hundreds. The waterfront is worth watching at any season. Directions by public transportation.

*** **Central Park** (862 acres) extends from 59th to 110th Streets, between Fifth and Eighth (Central Park West) Avenues. Most of the landbirds on our local list appear regularly in Central Park, an area of meadows, open parkland, woodland and thicket, murky ponds, a reservoir, and a growing clutter of buildings and roads. The Central Park list stands today at about 260 species, with a best one-day list of 101 species, including 29 warblers. The list of rarities includes the Purple Gallinule, Snowy Owl, Bewick's Wren, Townsend's Warbler, and Painted Bunting. Spring migrants with southern affinities regularly seen are the Blue-gray Gnatcatcher, Kentucky Warbler, and Orchard Oriole. Because of its light undergrowth this is one of the best areas for observing in spring such secretive birds as the Mourning Warbler and Lincoln's Sparrow.

(1) A favorite spot is the Ramble (opposite), between 72nd and 79th Streets, a neglected, hilly area where paths wind through groves of locust, willow, maple, birch, oak, and sycamore. (2) A small fenced-in Bird Sanctuary, near the southeastern corner at 59th Street and Fifth Avenue, has proved productive during migration time, particularly around the muddy panhandle of the lake. (3) The Reservoir at 90th Street is a haven from autumn to spring for loons, grebes, flocks of waterfowl, and gulls, including quite frequently a "white-winged" species. (4) The Loch, at 104th Street in the northwestern corner, is a marshy brook deep in a hollow surrounded by hardwoods.

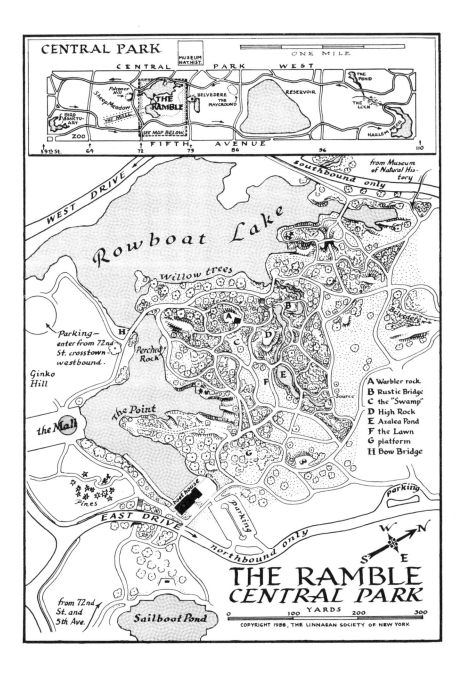

THE RAMBLE
CENTRAL PARK

A Warbler rock
B Rustic Bridge
C the "Swamp"
D High Rock
E Azalea Pond
F the Lawn
G platform
H Bow Bridge

YARDS

0   100   200   300

COPYRIGHT 1986, THE LINNAEAN SOCIETY OF NEW YORK

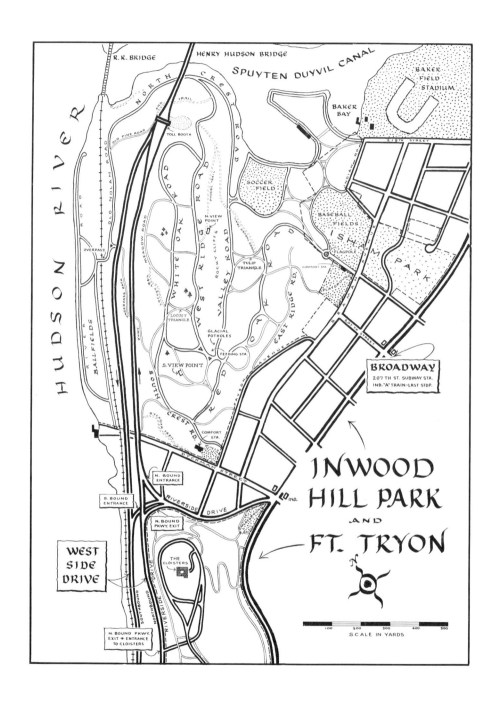

INWOOD
HILL PARK
AND
FT. TRYON

Public transportation: Madison Avenue bus and walk west one block, or IND 8th Avenue subway.

Other parks where regular watchers have compiled surprising lists over the years are:

* **Madison Square Park,** between East 23rd and East 25th Streets east of Fifth Avenue.

* **Trinity Churchyard,** Broadway and Wall Street.

* **St. Paul's Churchyard,** Broadway and Fulton Street.

* **Washington Square Park,** Fifth Avenue and 4th Street.

* **Bryant Park,** between West 40th and West 42nd Streets east of Avenue of the Americas.

* **Gramercy Park,** between East 20th and East 21st Streets east of Park Avenue (private, open to local residents only).

* **Carl E. Schurz Park,** between East 84th and East 89th Streets east of York Avenue.

* **Riverside Park,** along the Hudson River from West 72nd Street north to West 153rd Street.

** **Fort Tryon Park** (opposite) covers 61 acres between Henry Hudson Parkway and Broadway north of West 192nd Street. This park is largely natural woodland, excellent for warblers and other migrants in season. It has a breeding bird list more like that of the northern counties.

Public transportation: Madison Avenue bus No. 4 or IND 8th Avenue subway (Washington Heights line) to 190th or Dyckmann Street.

** **Inwood Hill Park** (opposite), east of Henry Hudson Parkway at West 207th Street, has natural woodland, which is attractive to migrants in season. This is Manhattan's highest elevation (405 feet) and a good vantage point for autumn flights of swifts, jays, thrushes, and hawks.

Public transportation: Madison Avenue bus No. 4 or IND 8th Avenue subway (Washington Heights line) to 207th Street.

* **Randalls Island Park,** in the East River. Consisting mostly of playing fields, it should be a haven for meadow birds and shorebirds in fall.

Public transportation: Bus to Long Island via Triborough Bridge.

Car: Triborough Bridge at East 125th Street and follow signs.

* **Wards Island Park,** in the East River. It has playing fields and a picnic grove; look for shorebirds and meadow birds in fall.

Public transportation: Bus to Long Island via Triborough Bridge, or footbridge from eastern end of 103rd Street.

Car: Triborough Bridge at East 125th Street and follow signs.

** **United Nations Promenade,** along the East River at East 47th Street. Iceland Gull is a regular visitant here in late winter and early spring.

** **Battery–Staten Island Ferry,** across the Upper Bay from the extreme southern tip of Manhattan to Staten Island. Formerly the Wilson's Petrel

BONAPARTE'S
GULL

occurred here in late summer, and may do so again. Look for the rare Little Gull in flocks of Bonaparte's Gulls here in April and May. At other times, loons, grebes, a variety of waterfowl, and other gulls may be seen from the ferry.

BROOKLYN, KINGS COUNTY: Like Manhattan, offers two basic habitats —parks and waterfronts.

*** **Prospect Park** (opposite) and the adjacent Brooklyn Botanic Garden, 600 acres, Flatbush Avenue south of Grand Army Plaza. The wooded hills, evergreen groves, ponds connected by winding brook, meadows, and landscaped areas, located along the Harbor Hill glacial moraine ridge, act as a migration flightline for hawks and smaller landbirds in spring and fall. Prospect Park boasts a list of more than 240 species, including many rarities. Suggested walk: from Flatbush Avenue bus stop go north through brushy area, rose garden, and Vale of Kashmir, cross East Drive, and follow the ridge line southwestward, around the Boulder Bridge to the Ravine, thence around Swan Boat Pond and Marsh, skirt the Quaker Cemetery, search Lookout Hill and the Point of the Lake, and then return to Three-Arch Bridge, the Bandstand Pond, and the wooded area just north.

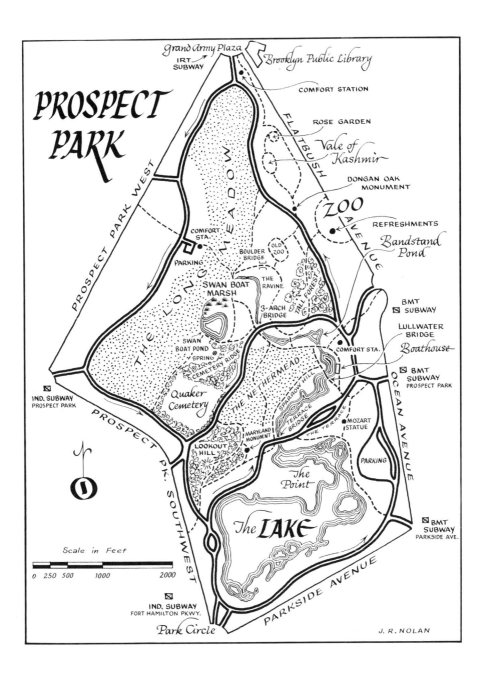

PROSPECT PARK

Grand Army Plaza

IRT SUBWAY

Brooklyn Public Library

COMFORT STATION

ROSE GARDEN

Vale of Kashmir

DONGAN OAK MONUMENT

ZOO

REFRESHMENTS

Bandstand Pond

FLATBUSH

PROSPECT PARK WEST

THE LONG MEADOW

COMFORT STA.

PARKING

BOULDER BRIDGE

OLD ZOO

THE RAVINE

TALL FOREST

SWAN BOAT MARSH

3-ARCH BRIDGE

BMT SUBWAY

LULLWATER BRIDGE

Boathouse

SWAN BOAT POND

SPRING

CEMETERY RIDGE

COMFORT STA.

BMT SUBWAY PROSPECT PARK

OCEAN AVENUE

AVENUE

IND. SUBWAY PROSPECT PARK

Quaker Cemetery

THE NETHERMEAD

SPARROW HILL

TERRACE BRIDGE

MOZART STATUE

THE TERRACE

PROSPECT PK. SOUTHWEST

MARYLAND MONUM'T

LOOKOUT HILL

PARKING

BMT SUBWAY PARKSIDE AVE.

The Point

The LAKE

Scale in Feet

0 250 500 1000 2000

IND. SUBWAY FORT HAMILTON PKWY.

Park Circle

PARKSIDE AVENUE

J. R. NOLAN

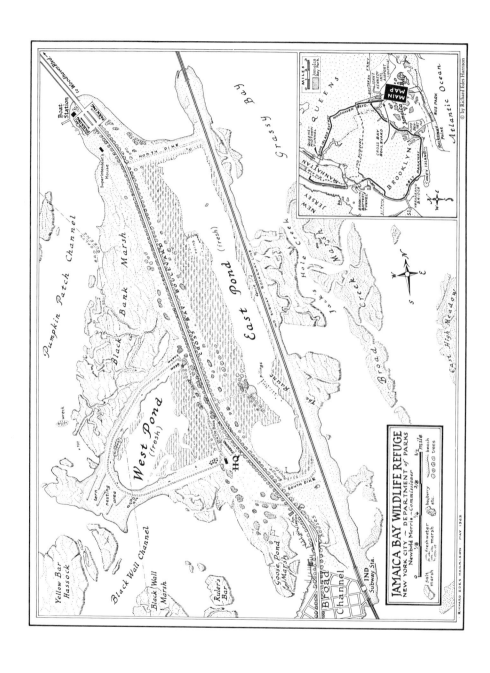

MAIN MAP

QUEENS

MANHATTAN

NEW JERSEY

BROOKLYN

Jamaica Bay Park

Atlantic Ocean

© by Richard Edes Harrison

Grassy Bay

Pumpkin Patch Channel

Black Bank Marsh

North Dike

Boat Station

Superintendent's House

West Pond (fresh)

East Pond (fresh)

Jacks Hole Creek

Broad Creek

Big Egg Marsh

East High Meadow

tern nesting area

wreck

HQ

South Dike

Goose Pond Marsh

Rider's Bar

Black Wall Marsh

Black Wall Channel

Yellow Bar Hassock

Broad Channel

IND Subway Sta.

JAMAICA BAY WILDLIFE REFUGE
NEW YORK CITY – DEPARTMENT of PARKS
Newbold Morris – Commissioner

0   1/8   1/4   3/8   1/2 mile

salt marsh   freshwater marsh   blueberry etc.   beach   trees

RICHARD EDES HARRISON MAY 1962

Public transportation: BMT Brighton Beach Express to Prospect Park Station, or IRT local to Grand Army Plaza.

Car: State Route 27 across Manhattan Bridge and straight out Flatbush Avenue.

** **Sewer Outfall at 91st Street.** The sewer no longer flows, but this spot still attracts gulls and it is a good vantage point for the Upper Bay of New York Harbor. All the common gulls may be seen from October to May, and just possibly such rare species as the Lesser Black-backed, Black-headed, and Little Gulls. Several species of terns may be seen in summer.

Public transportation: BMT Express, 4th Avenue line to end (95th Street), walk west to Shore Road, north to 91st Street, and cross footbridge to water.

Car: State Route 27A through Brooklyn-Battery Tunnel and along Shore Parkway to Exit 6, north on Shore Road to 92nd Street, park and walk.

* **Dyker Beach Park,** Shore Parkway at 87th Street. A rolling golf course, with woodland, and a tiny lake with marsh plants. Gulls move between the meadows and the ocean. A good area for migrant landbirds in autumn, meadow birds in winter.

Public transportation: BMT 4th Avenue line to 86th Street, walk east on 86th Street to Bay 7th Street entrance through clubhouse.

Car: Route 27A to Exit 7 at Bay 8th Street.

* **Coney Island** is our nearest to Times Square vantage point for pelagic species. An Ivory Gull was seen here in winter, 1964.

Public transportation: BMT Sea Beach Line to Stillwell Avenue. Walk south to beach.

Car: Route 27A to Exit 10, south on Ocean Parkway to beach.

* **Norton Point,** at the extreme western end of Coney Island. Landbirds in autumnal migration may be seen crossing the Narrows west to Staten Island, July through October, from this spot.

Public transportation: From Stillwell Avenue BMT station take Neptune Avenue bus to end.

Car: From Ocean Parkway, right on Neptune Avenue to end.

QUEENS COUNTY: New York City's largest county, bounded by water on the north, west, and south.

*** **Jamaica Bay Wildlife Refuge** (opposite), in Jamaica Bay. A man-made sanctuary with ponds, dikes, new plantings, salt marsh, and mud flats. This is worth a visit at any season; most exciting from July to October. Then concentrations of herons, gulls, terns, shorebirds, migrant landbirds are at their peak. In summer, breeding species include the Pied-billed Grebe, Glossy Ibis, Snowy and Common Egrets, Least Bittern, Green Heron, Common Gallinule, American Coot, and an amazing variety of waterfowl. Other breeding species include most of the birds from the Habitat M, S, and D lists, including the Bobwhite (introduced), possibly Traill's Flycatcher, and large colonies of Common Tern and Black Skimmer.

East Pond: In autumn, stand at the northwestern corner for a look south along the western edge of the pond for shorebirds — this is the most likely spot in our region for Avocet, Wilson's Phalarope, and Long-billed Dowitcher, and both godwits from August to October. West Pond: American Golden Plover regularly found, Baird's Sandpiper sometimes; the rare Buff-breasted Sandpiper is regular in the turf edging the pond. Search the pond for possible, but rare, phalaropes (northeastern corner preferred). In autumn, the refuge teems with terns, gulls, herons, swallows, and broods of local waterfowl; the plantings swarm with migrant landbirds. In winter, the site of the tern colony is an excellent spot for the Short-eared Owl, Ipswich Sparrow, and Lapland Longspur, and the ponds for waterfowl. A notebook with daily observations (not always reliable) is maintained near the parking lot. A permit to enter is required and is obtained from the New York City Department of Parks, Armory, Fifth Avenue at 64th Street.

Public transportation: IND Rockaway line to Broad Channel, walk north about 1 mile to entrance.

Car: State Route 27 or 27A to Cross Bay Boulevard, south on Cross Bay Boulevard, watch for sign on right at obscure entrance 1.4 miles south of first bridge. The refuge is conveniently near another fine area, Jacob Riis Park.

*** **Jacob Riis Park** (p. 66, inset) is on the south shore of Rockaway Peninsula. Fair in winter, good in spring, excellent in autumn. At that season it is best after a drop in temperature with northwest winds, especially when an early morning fog and onshore breezes pin down birds along the beach. Explore all the paths in the central mall area and walk east, circling the golf course; then the area around "the old army post" at the eastern end of the park. Leave the car at the western end of Neponset Avenue, walk through the fence, and search thoroughly all nearby bushes. In autumn this is the best place in the area for Blue Grosbeaks and Lark Sparrows. Fine in fall for landbirds, including rarities such as the Western Kingbird, Loggerhead Shrike, Philadelphia Vireo, Orange-crowned Warbler, Connecticut and Mourning Warblers, Dickcissel, and many flycatchers, jays, thrushes, tanagers, and finches. Watch for hawks streaking westward over the park in the fall. Excellent in late fall for winter finches.

Public transportation: IRT Flatbush Avenue to end, No. 935 bus to Fort Tilden.

Car: Route 27A (Shore Parkway) to Exit 15, south on Flatbush Avenue over Marine Parkway Bridge (toll). Leave car at extreme western end of parking field.

** **Breezy Point Park,** farther westward from Jacob Riis Park, is at the western end of Rockaway Peninsula. It is unfinished but should eventually equal Riis Park in merit. Entrance toll charged. The long rocky jetty is a recommended lookout for seabirds in winter.

* **Rockaway Beach,** between Beach 85th and Beach 95th Streets, is another convenient spot for pelagic birds. Strong southeast winds with rain in late May often bring Sooty Shearwaters close to the beach.

Car: Route 27A to Exit 15, south over Marine Parkway Bridge, west on Rockaway Point Boulevard to Breezy Point Park, east on Beach Channel Drive to Rockaway Beach.

* **John F. Kennedy International Airport** (p. 66, inset) is on the northeastern side of Jamaica Bay. Lawns, groves of evergreens, and ornamental pools in central mall attract landbirds in spring, autumn, and late autumn and hold them all day.

Car: Route 27 to Exit 24 or Van Wyck Expressway to Exit 1.

** **Forest Park** (538 acres) in mid-Queens is cut by Interborough Parkway, Woodhaven Boulevard, and Myrtle Avenue. This park, largely wooded and natural with maples, oaks, beech, and tulip trees, lies along the Harbor Hill glacial moraine ridge and is fine for landbirds on wave days in spring when the trees drip with warblers, vireos, and flycatchers. Best areas: along the railroad track on the western edge, along the south slope, around the golf course in the western section, and in the wedge-shaped sector north of Metropolitan Avenue on the eastern end.

MAGNOLIA
WARBLER

Public transportation: IND from Manhattan to Union Turnpike Station.

Car: Long Island Expressway (Int. Route 495) to Woodhaven Boulevard, right on Woodhaven Boulevard to Myrtle Avenue. Leave car south of park on Park Lane South.

* **Flushing Meadow Park,** site of 1964–65 World's Fair (to be developed).

The southern end around Willow Pond is now good for waterfowl, marsh birds, and occasionally for migratory landbirds.

Public transportation: IND Jamaica line to 75th Avenue Station.

Car: State Route 25 to 69th Road, east on 69th Road. Park on 69th Road or Jewel Avenue.

* **Kissena Park,** to the east in mid-Queens, has a small formal lake, the remnants of a tree nursery, a marshy southern end, and scrubby fields to the west, extending to Main Street and Queens Botanical Garden. Landbirds in season.

Car: North from the Long Island Expressway (Int. Route 495) on Kissena Boulevard.

** **Alley Pond Park** and **Alley Creek,** at the head of Little Neck Bay on the north shore, on both sides of Cross Island Parkway, has a variety of productive habitats. The steep wooded slope on the west side is excellent in spring.

Car to west side: Long Island Expressway (Int. Route 495) to exit on 231st Street, south on 233rd Street, which follows the park boundary. Entrances to "Big Woods" here, on 63rd Avenue, 230th Street, or 73rd Avenue.

East of Cross Island Parkway is a brackish pond and a creek with springs that attract landbirds all year. North of the railroad tracks are mud flats for shorebirds in the spring and fall. Here Green-winged Teal winter.

Car to east side: Take Grand Central Parkway to Alley Pond Park entrance; for the ponds and creek, drive north on Winchester Avenue (becomes Douglaston Boulevard). Park along Douglaston Boulevard to look over fresh-water marshes along Alley Creek. Continue north on Douglaston Boulevard, cross Long Island Expressway, go west on 53rd Avenue, park on 240th Street, and walk down the path to the marsh.

* **Douglaston Marsh,** north of the railroad, is attractive to shorebirds in spring and fall. North on Douglaston Boulevard to 235th Street, bear left to railroad station, park, and walk under the underpass and northwest toward the flats and marshes.

* **Oakland Lake Park,** northern Queens. There is a gully at the western end where wintering half-hardy birds may be found; a spring-fed marsh and thicket are at the eastern end. An attractive migration trap.

Car: Cross Island Parkway to Exit 5 (Northern Boulevard) or Bell Boulevard to 46th Street. Upper end: Park at eastern end of 46th Street or on Cloverdale Boulevard south from Northern Boulevard. By following Cloverdale south into Horatio, east on 50th Avenue, and then south on Hampton Boulevard, one parallels the often excellent park strip connecting with Alley Pond Park. Entrances along way.

* **Flushing Cemetery,** northeast of Kissena Park. A winter roosting area for owls and flocks of Mourning Doves, House Finches, and Cedar Waxwings.

Car: Long Island Expressway (Int. 495), north on 164th Street.

* **Mount St. Mary's Cemetery,** southeastern corner of Kissena Park at Fresh Meadow Road and North Hempstead Turnpike. For winter birds.

Car: Long Island Expressway (Int. 495) to 164th Street.

* **Crocheron Park,** west side of Little Neck Bay. A typical parkland with an overpass on its eastern end to the shore of Little Neck Bay. The Warbling Vireo is found nesting here.

Car: Clearview Expressway to 35th Avenue, east on 35th Avenue. For eastern end, park at foot of dead-end street on left, off 35th Avenue. For western end, park on 34th Avenue behind school.

* **Cunningham Park,** midway between Flushing Meadows and Alley Pond Parks and connected to Alley Pond Park by a bicycle path. It has a number of woodland ponds, and is — in places — excellent in spring and fall. Cut by highways (bounded on the east by Oceania Avenue and Hollis Court Boulevard, on the west by Francis Lewis Boulevard, on the north by Long Island Expressway, on the south by Grand Central Parkway) and split by Clearview Expressway and 73rd Avenue and Union Turnpike, making five major sections. The two sections north of 73rd Avenue are very good, but dry. The area south of 73rd and east of Hollis Court Boulevard is scrubby but often interesting. The woodland south of 73rd between Francis Lewis Boulevard and Clearview Expressway is also recommended; park west of Francis Lewis and walk through underpass.

Car: Grand Central Parkway to exit on Francis Lewis Boulevard.

The bays in northern Queens County are noted for waterfowl in winter with concentrations of Greater Scaup, Black Duck, Canvasback, Common Goldeneye, and Bufflehead:

* **Powell Cove,** west of Bronx-Whitestone Bridge.

Car: Whitestone Expressway (Int. 678) to Exit 2.

BUFFLEHEADS

* **Little Bay,** east of Throgs Neck Bridge.
Car: Cross Island Parkway to Exit 4.
* **Little Neck Bay,** east of Cross Island Parkway between Exits 4 and 5.
Car: Any roads reaching bay shore.

In southern Queens County are several areas of special interest in migration. The area is directly on a major migration route in spring, and every small plot can be productive:

* **Baisley Pond Park,** east of Baisley Boulevard in Ozone Park.
Car: Southern Parkway (Route 27) to Exit 25, north on Baisley Boulevard.
* **Springfield Park** and **Brookville Park** in Rosedale.
Car: For Springfield Park, Southern Parkway (Route 27) to Exit 28; south on Springfield Boulevard. For Brookville Park, North Conduit Boulevard (Route 27) south on Edgewood Avenue.
** **Spring Creek Park,** on the northern side of Jamaica Bay at Cross Bay Boulevard at 165th Street, is under development. Recommended in late summer and fall for the rarer meadow shorebirds — American Golden Plover, Upland Plover, Buff-breasted Sandpiper; in winter, for Short-eared Owl and Lapland Longspur.

THE BRONX: Despite its industrial clutter, the Bronx features some of our best parks, areas that have inspired a generation of bird watchers.

*** **Van Cortlandt Park** (opposite), 1132 acres, between 240th and 263rd Streets, east of Broadway. From the IRT Station at 242nd Street walk east across playing fields to the railroad tracks, turn north, cross Rowboat Pond, and enter a small wooded marsh bordering the golf course. Fish Crows, Rusty Blackbirds, and swallows are here in early spring; Wood Ducks, Traill's Flycatchers, Long-billed Marsh Wrens, Warbling Vireos, and other Habitat F species in the nesting season; possibly including Green Heron, Virginia Rail, and Sora. Common Snipe and Rusty Blackbird linger to early winter. The wooded slopes on the eastern side are Habitat W, excellent for spring migration and good in autumn; the Sycamore Swamp in the northeastern corner is fine for spring warblers, including the rarer species such as Golden-winged and Cerulean.

Public transportation: IRT 7th Avenue–Broadway line, to 242nd Street.
Car: Henry Hudson Parkway north to Exit 17 (Broadway), or Major Deegan Expressway to Van Cortlandt Park South Exit.
** **Bronx Park** (698 acres) has supurb aviaries and botanical gardens. It is north of 180th Street, west of Bronx River Parkway. An area of hilly woodlands, on both sides of the slow-moving Bronx River. The Hemlock Gorge along the river and the Hemlock Grove (about 40 acres) were formerly excellent for wintering owls and are still fine for birds that frequent conifers

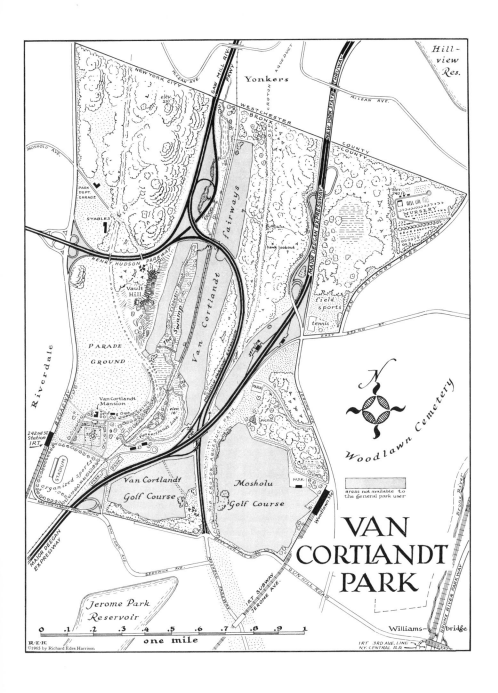

VAN CORTLANDT PARK

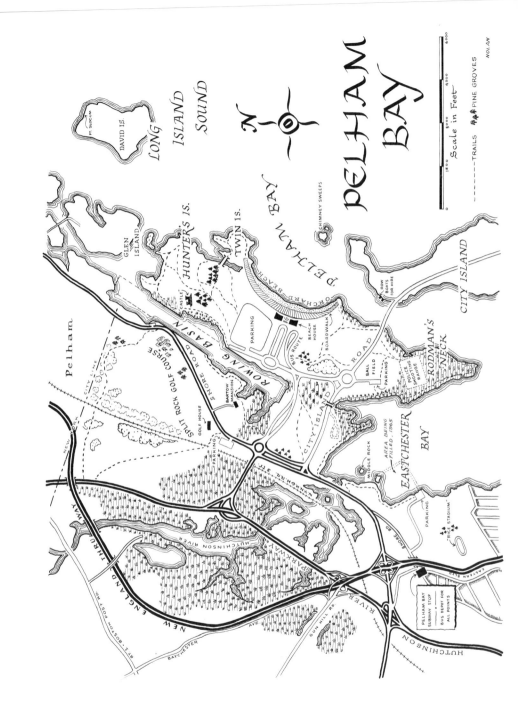

PELHAM BAY

Scale in Feet

0   1500   3000   4500   6000

----TRAILS   PINE GROVES

NOLAN

LONG   ISLAND   SOUND

DAVID IS.

FT. SLOCUM

N

GLEN ISLAND

HUNTERS IS.

TWIN IS.

CASTLE

CHIMNEY SWEEPS

PELHAM   BAY

ORCHARD BEACH

ROW BOATS FOR HIRE

CITY ISLAND

Pelham

NEW YORK

CITY LINE

SPLIT ROCK GOLF COURSE

SHORE ROAD

ROWING BASIN

BARTOW MANSION

GOLF HOUSE

PARKING

PARKING

BUS ROUTE

BEACH HOUSE

BOARDWALK

ROAD

PARKING

BALL FIELD

POLICE SHOOTING RANGE

RODMAN'S NECK

CITY ISLAND

MIDDLE ROCK

AREA BEING FILLED 1965

EASTCHESTER   BAY

NEW ENGLAND THRUWAY

RT. BOSTON POST RD.

HUTCHINSON RIVER

WINCHESTER ST.

HUTCHINSON RIVER PARKWAY

SHORE RD.

PARKING

RICE STADIUM

BATCHESTER AVE.

GUN HILL RD.

PELHAM BAY SUBWAY STOP

BUS DEPOT FOR ALL POINTS

EASTERN BLVD.

HUTCHINSON   RIVER

in winter. In the wooded area west of the river in the center of the park a Swainson's Warbler was discovered in April 1963.

Public transportation: IRT Lenox Avenue–Bronx line, to Bronx Park East, Pelham Parkway, or Allerton Avenue stations.

Car: Henry Hudson Parkway (State Route 9A) to Cross-Bronx Expressway (Int. Route 95), east on Cross-Bronx Expressway to Bronx River Parkway, north on Bronx River Parkway; or East River Drive to Bruckner Boulevard (State Route 1A) to Bronx River Parkway, north on Bronx River Parkway.

* **Jerome Park Reservoir** is between 197th and 238th Streets, east of Major Deegan Expressway. On one of the highest hills in the area and normally ice-free all winter. Several hundred ducks of a dozen species, including the Canvasback and Ruddy, rest here by day (usually at the north end) and fly out at dusk to feed in nearby bays and rivers.

Public transportation: IRT Lexington Avenue line to 125th Street, Jerome Avenue local to Mosholu Parkway Station, and walk west to Reservoir.

Car: Major Deegan Expressway north to 230th Street, east on 230th Street to Sedgwick Avenue, drive north, park along the northeastern or northwestern side of the reservoir, and view the reservoir from the playground at the north end.

*** **Pelham Bay Park** (opposite), in the northeastern corner of county on Long Island Sound, is the largest park in the county, a sprawling area of bay front, creek, meadows, salt marsh, woodland, and park. Fruitful in any season; best in winter. In the waters off Orchard Beach, Twin Islands, and the Lagoon in winter are Black Duck, American Widgeon, Canvasback, Common Goldeneye, Bufflehead, Red-breasted Merganser, and other waterfowl — Horned Grebe, occasionally loons, and rarely a Razorbill. In midwinter, Great Cormorants perch on the rocks of Twin Islands and Purple Sandpipers feed at water's edge. This is a favorite locale for owls, which require diligent searching. Look for Barred and Barn Owls in November in the upper (pine) or lower (spruce) groves on Hunter's Island; for Snowy and Short-eared around Rodman's Neck (also Red-tailed and Rough-legged Hawks); for Long-eared Owls in Hunter's Island groves all winter, and in the evergreens around the Bartow Mansion and around the edge of the golf course; for Saw-whet Owls in yews and cedars around Bartow Mansion. The Great Horned Owl bred in this area in 1965. Also look for the usual wintering park and meadow birds here, plus a better-than-average number of half-hardies.

Public transportation: IRT Lenox Avenue line, Pelham Bay Park local to terminus. Bus from Fordham Road and Grand Concourse.

Car: State Route 1A to Pelham Park Exit.

* **Ferry Point Park,** at the northern terminus of the Bronx-Whitestone

Bridge. A vantage point for waterfowl and gulls in winter; frequented in winter by such field birds as Short-eared Owl, Water Pipit, Horned Lark, Lapland Longspur, and Snow Bunting.

Car: First exit north of the tollgate.

* **Clasen Point,** on the East River, nearby. For waterfowl and gulls in winter; a scattering of shorebirds in fall.

Car: Bruckner Boulevard (Route 1A) to Sound View Avenue (just east of Bronx River Parkway), Sound View Avenue to end.

* **Throgs Neck** area, at the northern terminus of Throgs Neck Bridge. The fields and thickets here are interesting in autumn; in winter there are waterfowl in every cove and inlet.

Public transportation: IRT Lenox Avenue line, Pelham Bay Park local to terminus, bus from subway station.

Car: Bruckner Boulevard (Route 1A) to Tremont Street, south on Tremont Street to end.

STATEN ISLAND (opposite): New York's least populated county, the Borough of Richmond, has never had the intensive attention from bird watchers that the other boroughs have, and thus has fewer records of rarities. But situated as it is, between Long Island and New Jersey, it should be a migration trap for birds funneling down Long Island in autumn and pouring across from northern New Jersey in spring. Staten Island's ocean shore, facing southeastward, has a series of parks and vantage points from one end to the other. Bridges from New Jersey and Brooklyn; ferry from the Battery in Manhattan to St. George. All directions are from the Ferry terminal, at St. George.

*** **Great Kills Park** and **Oakwood Beach** are midway down the southeastern shore. Their best seasons are spring through autumn. In winter, many species of sea ducks may be found, as well as loons, grebes, gulls, and Purple Sandpiper; look for Short-eared Owls between the marina and Crookes Point at the southern end, from early November through March. In summer from the beach one may see terns, skimmers, and occasionally jaegers and Wilson's Petrels. In spring and fall, Oakwood Beach, just north of the park, has a good variety of shorebirds, a fair flight of hawks and other migrant landbirds.

Public transportation: SIRT to Oakwood Heights and walk east on Guyon Avenue, continue on Promenade or Fox Lane to beach; or bus No. 103 to park entrance on Hylan Boulevard. Walk south along waterfront to Crookes Point.

Car: East on Bay Street, south on Hylan Boulevard, left at Park entrance.

** **Wolfes Pond Park,** on the southeast shore just north of Princess Bay, has a little lake at the south end. Princess Bay has the only colony of Purple

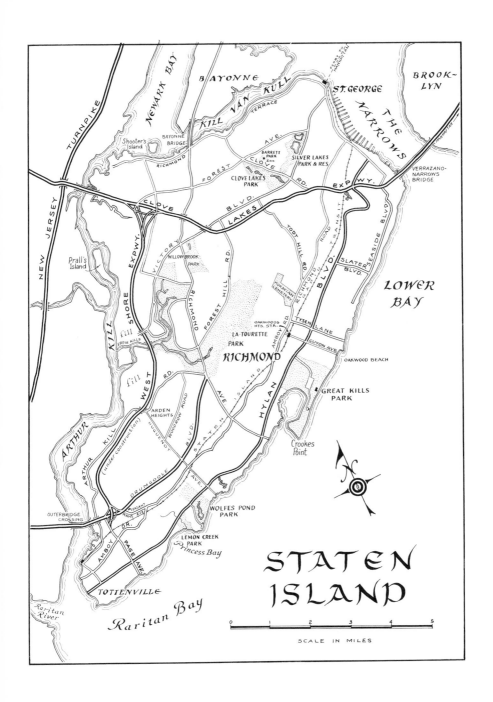

STATEN
ISLAND

SCALE IN MILES

Martins (60 pairs) in the city. Flocks of Bonaparte's Gulls may be seen here from September to April.

Public transportation: SIRT to Princess Bay, walk about one mile south on Seguine Avenue or take bus No. 115 or No. 116 to end. Walk north to park or south along the waterfront and adjacent streets to Tottenville.

Car: East on Bay Street, south on Hylan Boulevard to Princess Bay.

* **Tottenville,** on southern tip of island. There are two vantage points for seabirds in winter and during autumn migration here — at the southern end of Page Avenue and at the former site of the Russell Pavilion at the foot of Hylan Boulevard.

Car: East on Bay Street, south on Hylan Boulevard.

** **Fresh Kills,** midway on west side of island. These extensive marshes and dumps in winter are favored habitat for Rough-legged, Red-tailed, and Marsh Hawks, Short-eared Owl, and some of the rarer gulls.

Public transportation: Bus No. 108.

Car: South on Victory Boulevard (State Route 439A), left on State Route 440, right on Arthur Kill Road, right on Muldoon Avenue to Sanitation Department entrance.

Parks for spring landbird migration:

* **Clove Lakes Park,** about 2 miles south of St. George.

Car: Route 439A passes southern end.

* **Moravian Cemetery,** Dongan Hills.

Car: Route 439A to Todt Hill Road, east to cemetery.

* **New Springfield Park,** New Springfield. A small wildlife sanctuary not yet frequented by many birds.

Car: Route 439A to Travis Avenue, left on Travis Avenue into park.

** **Arden Heights.** The only Whip-poor-wills known to nest in the city call on summer evenings off Woodrow Road.

WHIP-POOR-WILL

Car: South on Route 439A, left on Route 440, right on Arthur Kill Road, left on Woodrow Road.

NASSAU COUNTY: On Long Island east of Queens County. This area has lost much of its semirural character since World War II. Gone is the remnant of prairie east of Hempstead and almost all traces of the wet woodlands that rimmed the southern shore. Farmlands have disappeared into featureless suburbia and all but gone are the breeding Upland Plovers, Bobolinks, and Vesper and Grasshopper Sparrows. Unless prompt conservation measures are taken, the vast wetlands that stretch across the south shore bays are doomed. The country north of the Jericho Turnpike (State Route 25) retains some of its rural aspect. Despite this disheartening prospect, no Nassau resident is very far from some area of protected greenery, water, or dunes, and the region remains one of the most fruitful for birds the year round. At Christmas time, watchers in northern and southern Nassau County regularly list more than 130 species (combined total) on their one-day counts. On a favorable May day, it is possible for one to record 150 or more species within the county.

Although much of the bird watching is limited to public parks and sanctuaries, there are still good areas in private or semipublic use. However, we do not recommend trespassing. When in doubt, ask permission.

Nassau County is good for spring migration — southward and westward for landbirds, southward for water and shorebirds — and exciting in summer and winter. In autumn, when weather conditions combine to "pin down" migrants along the outer beaches, phenomenal concentrations of species and numbers result. Following the passage of a cold front, with a northwest wind and a drop in temperature, good birding is probable; it can be sensational when accompanied in the early morning by fog and an offshore breeze. Then birds caught out over the water at dawn beat back and drop exhausted in the shrubbery of the south shore parks. Any mile of Nassau's southern boundary, a barrier beach from end to end, can be rewarding. The same beach can be productive in spring when an early morning fog follows a night flight.

*** **Atlantic Beach,** westernmost barrier beach with riprapped jetty. A favorite winter observation point for Common and Red-throated Loons, Horned and Red-necked Grebes, many species of gulls and sea ducks, and Purple Sandpipers. Such winter rarities as the Great Cormorant, Harlequin Duck, Common Eider, and the alcids regularly occur. Look for the same species on the waters of East Rockaway Inlet, south of the jetty, after winter storms. Although the jetty is private, there is no objection in winter to bird watchers who keep to the beach and avoid the clubhouse area. Warning: All jetties are slippery and dangerous in high seas or icy weather.

Public transportation: LIRR to Inwood Station and walk south on Doughty Boulevard for 2 miles, or LIRR to Far Rockaway Station and bus to Atlantic Beach, getting off where bus turns east after crossing Atlantic Beach Toll Bridge.

Car: State Route 27 to Exit 26, south on Rockaway Boulevard (State Route 104) to end, left on State Route 60, cross toll bridge to beach at 4th Street. Park at boardwalk and walk west to jetty.

*** **Lawrence Beach** and **Lawrence Marsh** (on the Peninsula, a noted spring migration funnel) lie north across Reynolds Channel from Atlantic Beach. There are landscaped estates surrounded by wetlands — creeks, salt marsh, and tidal flats — that have a long list of Habitat M breeding birds: American Bittern, Black Duck, Marsh Hawk, Clapper Rail, Long-billed Marsh Wren, Seaside and Sharp-tailed Sparrows. This is a busy feeding and resting ground for herons, waterfowl, and shorebirds, noted for rare visitants at all seasons, among them even Yellow Rail, Gyrfalcon, and Eared Grebe. Oak groves bordering suburban streets in this area are an excellent migration stopover for landbirds. Even the smallest patch of woodland catches migrants in May.

Car: Route 27, right on Rockaway Boulevard to its end (Meadow Lane), and then left on Causeway to (1) Sage Pond. In recent years the Least Bittern, Common Gallinule, and Virginia Rail have bred here. (2) At Causeway and Pond Crossing (Pond X) look for narrow lane (Mallow Way)

LEAST
BITTERN

leading to a dike that gives excellent views of the salt marsh. All six rails have been observed here, and four probably breed. (3) Hicks Beach, east of the dike, is a heronry accessible only by boat. (4) A driveway from Barret Road to yacht basin (western edge of golf course) gives access to another salt marsh and the waters of Bannister Creek, which are best for waterfowl in the colder months. Warning: The entire Lawrence Beach area seems badly tick-infested in spring and summer.

* **Woodmere Woods,** Hewlett. Although the famous woods are now largely destroyed or fenced, Peninsula area bird watchers still amass long lists from local gardens, parks, woodland remnants, golf courses, and bay shore. Two observers counted more than 100 species on one May day at Hewlett Harbor, just south of Hewlett. In fall and winter, brushy thickets and areas close to water give sanctuary to many half-hardy birds. House Finches are abundant.

Public transportation: LIRR to Hewlett.

Car: Route 27, right on Rockaway Boulevard, left on Peninsula Boulevard (State Route 2) to Mill Road.

*** **Point Lookout** is a residential community at the eastern end of the Long Beach strip — west of Jones Inlet, with its fast-moving current, rock jetties, and shoals. In recent winters this has been the best place for the Great Cormorant, Harlequin Duck, eiders, alcids, and rare gulls. In spring and fall the flats at low tide are shorebird havens. A Scissor-tailed Flycatcher appeared on this strip recently in autumn.

Public transportation: LIRR to Long Beach and bus to Point Lookout.

Car: East from Atlantic Beach; parking limited to Lido Boulevard. Parking is allowed in private driveways if requested politely. In winter, parking available at Hempstead Town Beach, just west of village.

*** **Jones Beach State Park** (p. 82) occupies 8 miles of barrier beach east of Jones Inlet. Excellent habitats include the parkways from the mainland, strand, dunes, fields, lawns, and plantings backed by creeks, bays, and salt marshes. Jones Beach has colonies of seabirds in summer, and pelagic species — shearwaters, jaegers, and petrels — to be seen from the beaches. Migrating landbirds are everywhere in autumn, under conditions described on page 79. A day in late September, with 250,000 swallows boiling through the air, with flickers, jays, doves, hawks, and dozens of other species of landbirds crowding into every cover, will never be forgotten. Early morning hours are best.

Worthwhile locations: (1) Short Beach, at the eastern end on Jones Inlet. For ducks and other seabirds. Rarities in recent winters here include both eiders, Black-legged Kittiwake, Little Gull, Razorbill, Common Murre, Black Guillemot. Purple Sandpiper is regular visitant in winter; Dunlin and Sanderling most winters. Park in West End Parking Field 2 and walk west to

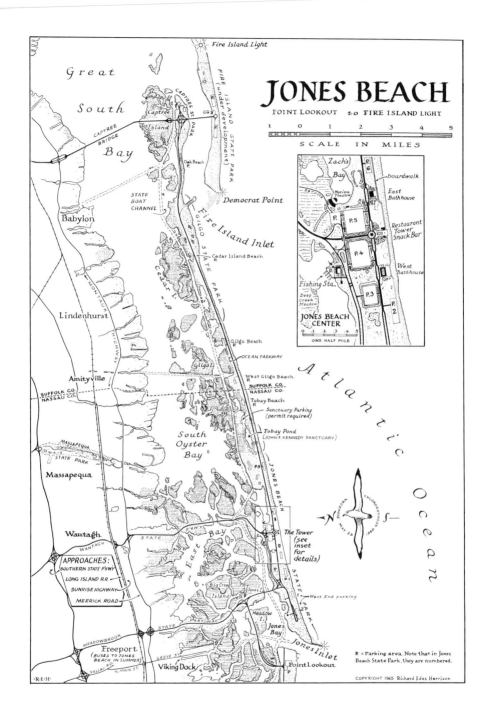

JONES BEACH

POINT LOOKOUT *to* FIRE ISLAND LIGHT

SCALE IN MILES

R = Parking area. Note that in Jones Beach State Park, they are numbered.

COPYRIGHT 1965 Richard Edes Harrison

jetty. (2) Search the pine groves east of West End Parking Field 1 for Saw-whet Owls and other owls in winter. (3) Scan the dunes between Parking Field 1 and jetty for Snowy Owls in winter. (4) Examine West End Parking Field 1 and lawns adjacent to it for Horned Larks and Snow Buntings. (5) The plantings around the police barracks and superintendent's houses are excellent for landbirds in autumn, but one must have permission to walk about. (6) The junction of Meadowbrook State Parkway and Ocean Parkway has Common Tern, Black Skimmer, and Piping Plover nesting colonies. Drive slowly and do not enter the nesting grounds. (7) *** The Fishing Station, on the channel side opposite Parking Field 4, has a large service garage well landscaped with sycamores, evergreens, and beach plum. A walk or two around this building in fall may produce a surprising list of landbirds. Rarities such as the Western Tanager and Dickcissel have been seen here. (8) The pine plantings around Parking Field 4 (open all year) are just east. (9) *** Zach's Bay is a fine area east of Parking Area 5 on the channel side. (In off season, walk from northeastern corner of Parking Field 4.) Search lawns and plantings for landbirds in autumn. Orange-crowned, Connecticut, and Mourning Warblers can be found; one year a Golden-crowned Sparrow turned up. Survey the beach and waters of Zach's Bay for shorebirds and water birds. Look for redpolls, crossbills, and siskins in evergreens in winter. (10) The entire beach strip is a hawk flightline in autumn — mostly Marsh Hawks, Ospreys, and falcons headed westward. During reverse migration (sea to land) search around buildings and the central water tower for injured birds; and wires, light poles, and dune tops for shrikes, hawks, and other rarities.

Car: Route 27 to Meadowbrook State Parkway, south to Ocean Parkway, east or west along the beach.

*** **John F. Kennedy Memorial Wildlife Sanctuary** (opposite), east of Jones Beach. Parking area, observation tower, and paths. Required is an entrance permit from the Town Clerk, Town of Oyster Bay, Long Island, which maintains the sanctuary. The sanctuary is closed to all during the duck hunting season. It centers on a shallow, brackish pond, about 3500 feet long, surrounded by phragmites and spartina and, on the north side, high dunes. The pond is a mecca for migrating and wintering water birds and waterfowl. The margins of the pond attract many migrating shorebirds in autumn. Rare but possible are: Ruff, all three phalaropes, American Golden Plover, Baird's Sandpiper, and all the larger species — Willet, Hudsonian and Marbled Godwits, and Whimbrel. Black and Forster's Terns are regular visitants in September. At this season migrant landbirds throng among the bayberry, poison ivy, pitch pine, and wild cherry habitat on the dunes. The observation tower is convenient for watching the migration of hawks, swallows, and smaller landbirds in autumn. Northwest of the pond is a heronry where Common and Snowy Egrets, Little Blue and Green Herons, and Black-crowned and Yellow-crowned Night Herons have nested. Louisiana Herons may nest near the pond.

Car: East from Jones Beach, enter Tobay Beach Parking Field, drive to the access road at the southwestern corner and follow to parking area at end, then walk west.

** **South Oyster Bay.** Between the barrier beach and island mainland are many bays, creeks, and channels, mostly inaccessible except by boat. Noteworthy waterfowl concentrations are found here in winter, particularly of Brant, reaching a total of 25,000 — 30,000 in recent winters. Their constantly shifting flocks gather in bays from Jamaica Bay to South Oyster Bay, and may be seen from many adjacent shore points.

* **Valley Stream State Park,** in Valley Stream, in the interesting southwestern Nassau County area, often has waterfowl in winter; the woodland at the northern end is occasionally productive.

Car: From Exit 34 on Laurelton Parkway (Belt System), east on Merrick Road, north on Franklin Avenue to West Dover or West Chester Streets.

*** **Hempstead Lake State Park** (opposite), in south-central Nassau County, has a long record of productivity. This 3-mile strip runs north and south and is cut by three east-west highways. (1) At the northern end, north of Southern State Parkway, an open area, woodlands, stream, and the marshy northern end of Hempstead Reservoir repay search in any season, especially for wintering half-hardy species and the shier river ducks. (2) Hempstead Reservoir is south of Southern State Parkway. From autumn to spring, except when frozen over, numbers of Mallard, Black Duck, Gadwall, American Widgeon, Pintail, Green-winged Teal, Greater and Lesser Scaups, Canvasback, Common Goldeneye, Ruddy Duck, Common Merganser, and other species can be found. Below the dam on the southern end of the Reservoir is a wooded area with a fenced-in bird sanctuary on the western side which is good in spring for warblers, as well as for Pied-billed Grebes and Wood Ducks. Kentucky, Prothonotary, and Yellow-throated Warblers have been seen here in recent springs. The South Pond occasionally harbors waterfowl, and rarely a shorebird. (3) The wooded strip west of Lynbrook Spur of Peninsula Boulevard between Ocean Avenue and Lakeview Avenue (along the aqueduct) may be flooded with migrants on "wave" days in spring. (4) Smith Pond, farthest south in Rockville Centre, is noted for the variety of its waterfowl — including Hooded Merganser, Ring-necked Duck, and occasionally a Redhead.

Public transportation: LIRR to Rockville Centre, walk west on Merrick Road to Smith Pond and work north.

Car: Southern State Parkway to North Village Avenue Exit (19). Park on North Village Avenue, opposite riding stables for the northern section;

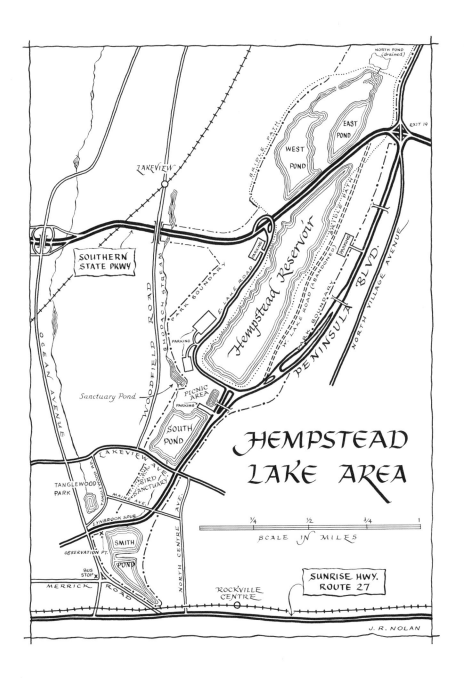

NORTH POND (drained)

EXIT 19

LAKEVIEW

BRIDLE PATH

WEST POND

EAST POND

SOUTHERN STATE PKWY

Hempstead Reservoir

PARKING

WOODFIELD ROAD

SHODACH STREAM

PARK BOUNDARY

E. LAKE ROAD

W. LAKE ROAD (ABANDONED)

PARK BOUNDARY

WATER PATH

PARKING

PENINSULA BLVD.

NORTH VILLAGE AVENUE

PARKING

Sanctuary Pond

PICNIC AREA

PARKING

OCEAN AVENUE

SOUTH POND

HEMPSTEAD
LAKE AREA

LAKEVIEW AVE.

BIRD SANCTUARY

TANGLEWOOD PARK

MAINE AVE.

TANGLEWOOD ROAD

LYNBROOK SPUR

NORTH CENTRE AVE.

¼   ½   ¾   1

SCALE IN MILES

OBSERVATION PT.

SMITH POND

BUS STOP

MERRICK   ROAD

ROCKVILLE CENTRE

SUNRISE HWY.
ROUTE 27

J. R. NOLAN

off the peripheral parkway for the reservoir; off Lynbrook Spur at the sail-
boat pond for the sanctuary; on side streets off Lynbrook Spur for Smith
Pond.

Other convenient areas in southern Nassau County:

** Meadowbrook State Parkway, between Southern State Parkway
and Sunrise Highway (Route 27). Southern (Freeport) end for landbirds
in spring and fall. Park on Babylon Turnpike where it crosses parkway. The
Parkway strip is also excellent north at Smart's Pond in Roosevelt.

* Wantagh State Park, cut by Sunrise Highway between Wantagh and
Bellmore. Three reservoirs, surrounded by woods and bordered in places
with marshes.

* Massapequa State Park (p. 82), cut by Southern State Parkway,
Sunrise Highway (Route 27), and Merrick Road, east of Massapequa. A
typical pine-oak scrub in the northern section; Lake Massapequa south of
Clark Street.

** Tackapausha Preserve (65 acres) is the southern part of Massapequa
State Park, south of Sunrise Highway. A county-operated wildlife sanctuary,
with a museum, nature trails, forest, pond, and brackish marsh. It has an
excellent breeding-bird list. Entrance on Sunrise Highway, Massapequa.

EASTERN
BLUEBIRD

Northern Nassau County, particularly eastward, remains estate country.
Here in meadowland and orchard, Eastern Bluebird, Vesper and Grasshopper Sparrows still breed. During spring migrations, almost any woodland with flowing water is favorable, and in autumn and winter brushy
thickets and protected lowlands should be searched. In spring, the east-
facing slopes, with their morning sunshine, are most attractive to birds.

*** **Mill Neck,** an estate community west of Oyster Bay, is entirely a bird sanctuary. Here rolling hills slope to a river valley that drains through a lake into Mill Neck Bay. (1) Typical salt-creek habitat in the bay, with herons, waterfowl, shorebirds, rails, and gulls in season; a pair of breeding Ospreys in summer. (2) South of the dam on Cleft Road, Beaver Lake has waterfowl in the colder seasons. (3) South of the railroad embankment at the southern end of the lake is a marshy estuary with breeding records of the Least Bittern, Wood Duck, Virginia Rail, Belted Kingfisher, and other Habitat F species. (4) South of the estuary is a magnificent wet woodland of oak, beech, maple, and towering tulip trees. The whole area is exciting at the peak of spring migration; but is especially favored in April for early Eastern Phoebe, swallows, Palm Warbler, and Purple Finch. Wood Duck, Broad-winged and Red-shouldered Hawks, Yellow-throated Vireo, and Louisiana Waterthrush breed in this area.

Public transportation: LIRR to Mill Neck, walk west along railroad embankment or take encircling roads. (Warning: Be alert for trains!) For the woodland, walk south on Mill Neck Road for 200 yards and west on Shu Swamp Road, to the bridge.

Car: Hempstead Turnpike (State Route 25A), north on Wolver Hollow Road, right on Chicken Valley Road, right on Glen Cove Road, left on Mill Neck Road to the station; or from Oyster Bay village west on West Main Street and left on Cleft Road to dam.

Vantage points on Long Island shore for seeing migrating and wintering loons, grebes, geese, ducks, cormorants, terns, and gulls:

* **Sands Point** is on Long Island Sound. North from Sands Point Village on Middle Neck Road.

* **Morgan Memorial Park** is on the east shore of Hempstead Harbor. West from Glen Cove on Landing Road.

* **Dosoris Island** has a pond and stream. West from Lattingtown on Lattingtown Avenue.

* **Oak Neck Beach** provides marshlands. North of Bayville.

* **Roosevelt Memorial Park,** Oyster Bay.

* **Roosevelt Sanctuary** (12 acres), at Oyster Bay, has a small museum and more than 40 breeding species on well-planted grounds. Open summer months only.

Car: East from Oyster Bay village on East Main Street for about 1 mile.

** **Mill Pond,** Oyster Bay. A swampy woodland south of the small pond is attractive in early spring. Pied-billed Grebe, Blue-winged Teal, Wood Duck, Yellow-bellied Sapsucker, swallows, and Rusty Blackbird often appear here earlier than elsewhere.

Car: West on West Main Street to Lake Avenue, left for 300 yards.

SUFFOLK COUNTY: Our biggest, most diverse county, with a host of fine bird-watching areas. The bird watching is better here in autumn and winter than in spring. The south shore from Tobay Beach to Montauk is all worthwhile, being a continuation of the barrier beaches of Nassau County.

** **Gilgo Beach** (p. 82), a settlement of cottages some 2 miles east of Tobay Beach on the barrier island, is a noted migration trap in autumn. Search all around the cottages for flycatchers, thrushes, vireos, warblers, and occasionally Lark and Lincoln's Sparrows. The beach stretches eastward for miles, with dunes to the south and salt marsh and tidal flats to the north. Look for Rough-legged Hawk, Short-eared and Snowy Owls in winter, gull, tern, and skimmer colonies in summer.

Car: Ocean Parkway east, park in Gilgo village parking lot, walk east to pine groves and lawns of former Coast Guard Station, a brick structure south of highway.

*** **Oak Beach** (p. 82), on the barrier beach facing Fire Island Inlet. Good for shorebirds in migration; seabirds in winter.

Car: Ocean Parkway east of Gilgo Beach.

** **Captree State Park** (p. 82), at the eastern tip of the barrier island. Best in autumn; good in summer and winter. After summer or tropical storms, during autumn migration, and during winter watch for stray pelagics — shearwaters, jaegers, phalaropes, seabirds, and shorebirds. This is a landbird trap in autumn.

Car: East on Ocean Parkway from Oak Beach to end, or south from State Route 27A on Captree Causeway, left on Ocean Parkway to entrance.

*** **Fire Island** (31 miles long) is the easternmost barrier island, with roads only at both ends. (1) *** Fire Island State Park (p. 82) has a channel-side salt marsh with typical species and an oceanfront jetty attractive to eiders, Harlequin Duck, and Purple Sandpiper in winter. Outstanding for its landbird migration in autumn. (2) * Sunken Forest is a private sanctuary between Point O' Woods and Cherry Grove. Here is a magnificent dense forest of black and post oaks, pitch pine, red cedar, wild cherry, American holly, and tangles of wild grape, catbrier, and poison ivy. Interesting in autumn and winter for landbirds. Walk east from Cherry Grove. (2) * Suffolk County Park Beach is an ocean vantage point near the east end.

Public transportation: Ferry from Bay Shore to Kismet, Fair Harbor, Ocean Beach, Ocean Bay Park, and Point O' Woods (private); from Sayville to Cherry Grove and Fire Island Pines; and from Patchogue to Davis Park.

Car: Bridge from Oak Beach on Ocean Parkway to Fire Island State Park. South from Montauk Highway (State Route 27) on William Floyd Parkway to Suffolk County Beach Park.

*** **Moriches Bay** and **Inlet,** feature a wide shallow bay with sandbars and broad tidal flats, protected from the sea by an outer beach through which a narrow inlet flows. The area is famous for colonies of terns and skimmers in summer; shorebirds and storm-borne exotics in spring and autumn, waterfowl in winter. Best "worked" from a rowboat, with or without a motor. Look for shorebirds, terns, skimmers and other water birds on and around the largest island in the bay; 20 or more species on a good day — including the larger shorebirds such as the Whimbrel, Willet, Hudsonian and Marbled Godwits, and many smaller species. Breeding birds include Piping Plover, Common and Least Terns, Black Skimmer, and American Oystercatcher. Moriches Inlet is especially good for the rare southern terns (Gull-billed, Royal, Sooty, Caspian) and wanderers — it has produced such species as White-tailed Tropicbird, White-bellied Booby, Magnificent Frigatebird, and White Ibis.

Car for Moriches Bay area: Route 27 to East Moriches, where rowboats are available for about $4 per day, including tow out and back.

Car for Inlet: Route 27 to Westhampton, south across the bridge to barrier beach, west on Dune Road to end.

* **Eastport,** good pond for ducks, on the grounds of the Long Island Country Club, is about 0.5 mile north of Route 27.

* **Westhampton Beach Village** is south of Westhampton on Hill Road. Search the golf links for crossbills in winter. A cranberry bog, at the northeastern village limits north to State Route 27, is a habitat for Wood Duck, Ring-necked Duck, and Hooded Merganser in winter.

*** **Shinnecock Bay** and **Inlet** (p. 90) are south of Hampton Bays. This marine bay is sheltered by barrier beach, with access to the sea through a narrow inlet. The sandbars a few hundred yards from the inlet are sometimes very good for shorebirds and southern wanderers; they are best approached by rowboat. Nesting Great Black-backed and Herring Gulls frequent the islands at the Inlet; the Least Tern and Piping Plover nest on Shinnecock Beach, as well as Spotted Sandpiper, American Oystercatcher,

HERRING
GULLS

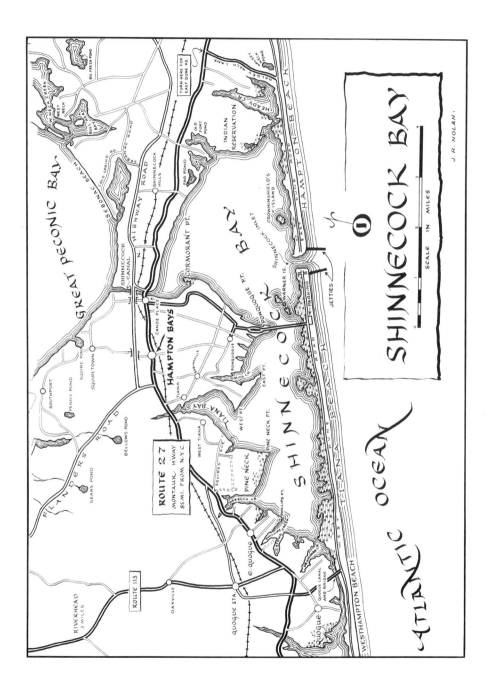

SHINNECOCK BAY

SCALE IN MILES

J. R. NOLAN.

and Prairie Horned Lark. The beach is excellent for Snowy and Short-eared Owls in flight years; and is a regular location for the Purple Sandpiper. Look seaward for shearwaters and jaegers in late summer. A birdbanding project on Tiana Beach, on the barrier beach near the Tiana Coast Guard Station just west of Inlet, banded in six autumns more than 22,000 birds of 131 species, including 30 species of warblers and rarities such as Sage Thrasher, Bell's Vireo, Prothonotary Warbler, Yellow-throated Warbler, Blue Grosbeak, Lark Sparrow, and Clay-colored Sparrow!

Car: South from Route 27 at Canoe Place on Lynn Avenue to end, west on Dune Road to Tiana Beach, east on Dune Road to Inlet and jetties; or south from Southhampton on Halsey Neck Lane to Dune Road and west to Inlet and jetties.

*** **Mecox Bay** and **Inlet** (p. 92, inset), south of Water Mill on Route 27. Flocks of Canada Geese winter on the bay or in rye fields nearby. The Whistling Swan appears regularly in autumn. Another excellent shorebird location. The Black-necked Stilt was recorded here once. A good variety of marine water birds winter here.

Car: South from Route 27 on Flying Point Road to end; or south from Hayground on Mecox Road, south on Job's Lane, west on Dune Road to inlet.

Other excellent areas on the south shore (p. 92, inset):

** **Mill Pond,** north of Route 27 at Water Mill, for wintering waterfowl, particularly Redhead and Ring-necked Ducks.

** **Sagaponack Pond,** south from Bridgehampton on Atlantic Avenue, east on Bridge Lane.

** **Wainscott Pond,** southwest of Wainscott.

** **Kellis Pond,** south of Route 27 between Hayground and Bridgehampton. The American Golden Plover is regularly found in fields from Mecox Bay east to Wainscott in autumn.

** **Georgica Pond,** east of Wainscott.

** **Hook Pond,** south of East Hampton, harbors Canada Geese, with occasionally a few Snows and Blues, and one or two European Widgeon in winter. The sanctuary along the stream at the north end often has wintering landbirds.

*** **Montauk Peninsula** (p. 92) is at the easternmost tip of Long Island, and is the county's most famous bird-watching spot. There is no better place in winter for seeing the Common and Red-throated Loons, Red-necked and Horned Grebes, Gannet, Great Cormorant, sea ducks such as eiders and the Red-breasted Merganser, "white-winged" gulls, Black-legged Kittiwake, Bonaparte's and other gulls, and particularly members of the alcid family. Every part of the 14-mile stretch from Amagansett east is inter-

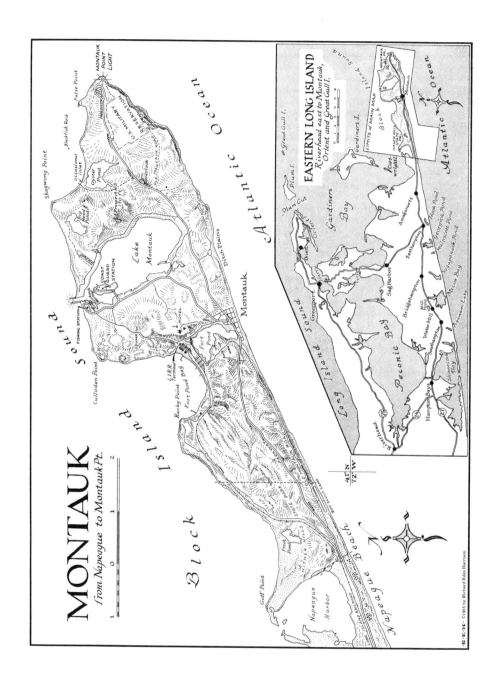

MONTAUK
from Napeague to Montauk Pt.

Atlantic Ocean

Block Island Sound

Block Island Sound

MONTAUK POINT LIGHT

Montauk Point

False Point

Blackfish Rock

Shagwong Point

U.S. MILITARY RESERVATION

OCCASIONAL INLET

Oyster Pond

Big Reed Pond

Prospect Hill
170 ft.

Overlook

OLD MONTAUK HIGHWAY

Lake Montauk

Culloden Point

COAST GUARD STATION

FISHING STATION

Ditch Plains

Montauk

Rocky Point Terminal

L.I.R.R.

Fort Pond

Fort Pond Bay

Hither Woods

Goff Point

Napeague Harbor

Fresh Pond

HITHER HILLS STATE PARK

MONTAUK STATE PARKWAY

LONG ISLAND RAILROAD

Napeague Beach

·R·E·H· ©1965 by Richard Edes Harrison

EASTERN LONG ISLAND
Riverhead east to Montauk, Orient and Great Gull I.

Long Island Sound

Great Gull I.

Little Gull I.

Plum I.

Plum Gut

Orient

Gardiners I.

Gardiners Bay

Fort Wright

Peconic Bay

Greenport

Sag Harbor

Amagansett

Napeague Bay

Block Island Sound

MONTAUK

Montauk

HITHER HILLS STATE PARK

LIMITS OF MAIN MAP

Fresh Pond

Georgica Pond

Wainscott Pond

Sagaponack Pond

Mecox Bay

Agawam Lake

Shinnecock Bay

Hampton Bays

Water Mill

Mill

Southampton

Bridgehampton

Easthampton

Riverhead

Atlantic Ocean

41°N
72°W

N

WHITE-WINGED
CROSSBILL

esting at this season; several parts are exceptional. (1) Montauk Point: Park at the end of Route 27, and search the pine groves for Saw-whet Owls and crossbills. Then walk to the buffs beside the lighthouse and scan the ocean; then to the stony beach northwestward to Shagwong Point. In winter look for eiders and Harlequin Duck; also possible are the Razorbill, Thick-billed Murre, Dovekie, and Black Guillemot. At times thousands of scoters of all three species winter off the point. Red-breasted Merganser is probably the next most abundant duck. From August 15 to November 15, shearwaters, jaegers, petrels, terns, phalaropes, and other offshore species sometimes skirt the point in their southward migration. Walking across the moors in winter will bring one to stunted oak woods in glacial kettleholes and to dense thickets where half-hardy birds find shelter. East Lake Drive, on the east side of Lake Montauk, leads to the highest hills in the area, and east of these is Oyster Pond, a duck haven when ice-free, and Big Reed Pond, surrounded by marshes. Watch the wires for Sparrow Hawk and Northern Shrike; the hills for Red-tailed and Rough-legged Hawks; the lowland marshes for Marsh Hawk and Short-eared Owl; and the dunes for Snowy Owl. Two jetties at the northern end of Lake Montauk, on West Lake Drive, are favored locations for the Common Loon, Great Cormorant, Harlequin Duck, and Purple Sandpiper. (2) ** Montauk village: Fort Pond, north of Montauk Parkway (State Route 27); the Ditch Plains Coast Guard Station, south of Route 27; the shrubbery and plantings anywhere, but especially around Montauk Manor (hotel). (3) * Hither Hills State Park, cut by Route 27 about 4 miles west of Montauk, a beautiful area with white sand dunes, pine woods, a fresh-water lake. (4) The campground, on the shore road (Old Montauk Road), is

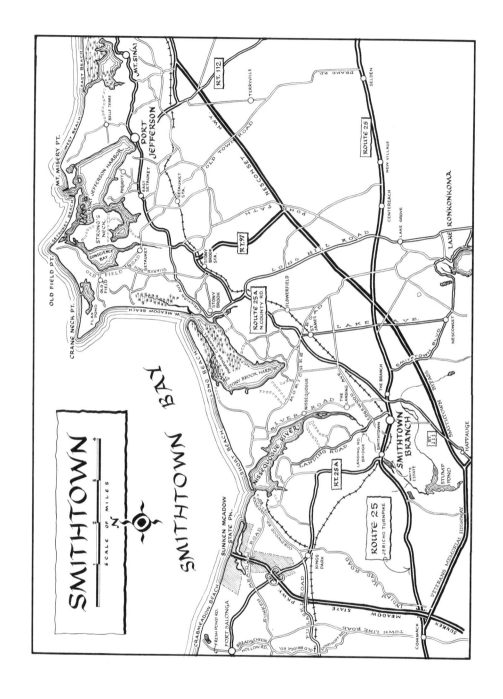

excellent for Horned Larks, Snow Buntings, and Lapland Longspurs in winter. (5) Lazy Point Road north from Route 27 leads to Goff Point, an observation point for watching the large flocks of Common Goldeneye, Old-squaw, Bufflehead, and Red-breasted Merganser in ** Napeague Harbor in winter.

** **Acabonack Harbor,** east of Springs, has breeding Bank and Rough-winged Swallows and a few pairs of Ospreys.

** **Morton National Wildlife Refuge,** on Jessup's Point north of Noyack, has Red-tailed Hawk and Great Horned Owl breeding in Noyack Woods just to the south.

* **Scallop Pond,** on Cow's Neck northwest of North Sea village, has waterfowl.

The north shore, largely bluffs and narrow beaches, though not as spectacular, can be most rewarding, especially in the harbors and inlets.

* **Caumsett State Park** (undeveloped) is on Lloyd's Neck north of Cold Spring Harbor. It is a good spot in autumn and winter for Red-tailed and Rough-legged Hawks. Permission to enter must be obtained from Superintendent, Long Island State Park Commission Headquarters; telephone, 516 MO 9-1000.

Car: North from State Route 25A from Cold Spring Harbor.

** **Huntington.** The Warbling Vireo, a Long Island rarity, breeds at intersection of Route 25A and Park Avenue.

Car: East from Huntington on Route 25A to Park Avenue.

* **Cold Spring Harbor State Fish Hatchery,** at the head of Cold Spring Harbor. The woods around the ponds, which are on the east side of State Route 108, north of the hatchery, have breeding Rough-winged Swallows, Yellow-throated Vireos, and Louisiana Waterthrushes.

* **Fresh Pond,** Fort Salonga (opposite). Breeding Habitat F and M species and possibly Wood Duck and Virginia Rail. Private, viewed from road.

Car: North from Fort Salonga on Fresh Pond Road.

* **Sunken Meadow State Park** (opposite), on Long Island Sound north of Kings Park, has breeding rails, wintering waterfowl, and in winter, hawks, Horned Larks, and Snow Buntings. A good vantage point for water birds is at the mouth of the Nissequogue River at the foot of Old Dock Road on the west side of the Kings Park Hospital.

Car: Park entrance on Route 25A just west of Kings Park.

*** **Nissequogue River** (opposite), at Smithtown. (1) Two ponds in the headwaters: one on the White estate just south of Route 25A has river ducks regularly in fall — Gadwall, Ring-necked, Redhead, Ruddy Duck, and Hooded Merganser; Stump Pond (New Mill Pond), farther south, east of Willett's Old Path, is a wild area with marshes and woodlands. Although

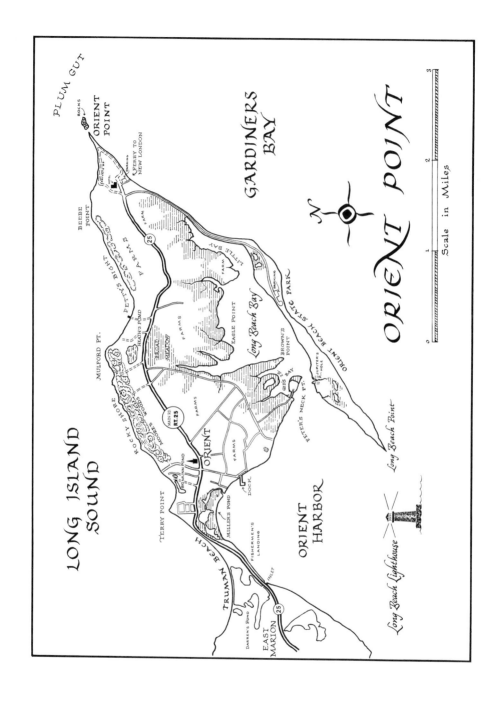

ORIENT POINT

PLUM GUT

ROCKS

ORIENT POINT

FERRY TO NEW LONDON

PARKING

HOTEL

PRIVATE

BEEBE POINT

PETTY'S BIGHT

FARMS

FARM

LITTLE BAY

MULFORD PT.

BEACH'S POND

FARMS

EAGLE POINT

Long Beach Bay

GARDINERS BAY

ROCKY SHORE

WOODS

PEAT MEADOW

FARMS

BROWN'S POINT FARM

PARKING

ORIENT BEACH STATE PARK

MAIN RD. RT. 25

FARMS

BEN JONN POND

ORIENT

FARMS

GULLS BAY

JUPITER'S HOLE

N

LONG ISLAND SOUND

BROOKS

PETER'S NECK PT.

25

TERRY POINT

DOCK

MILLER'S POND

ORIENT HARBOR

Long Beach Point

FISHERMEN'S LANDING

TRUMAN BEACH

INLET

25

DARBY'S POND

EAST MARION

Long Beach Lighthouse

Scale in Miles

0 1 2 3

private at present, the county may purchase the property and maintain it as a nature preserve. (2) The white bridge, north from Route 25 just east of Smithtown Branch on Landing Road (harbor road), looks out on cattail marshes bordered by wooded hillsides. In late autumn and early winter this area holds the Eastern Phoebe, Winter and Carolina Wrens, Myrtle Warbler, Catbird, Robin, and Golden-crowned Kinglet; also wintering blackbirds, finches, sparrows, and hawks. (3) River Road, north from Route 25A just east of Smithtown Branch, is good for wintering bay ducks; look for the Brown Creeper, Eastern Bluebird, and Cedar Waxwing in the woods. Follow the left fork to Short Beach, a lookout for wintering seabirds; or the right fork to Long Beach for a view of waterfowl on the Sound.

* **Conscience Bay** (p. 94), in Stony Brook Harbor north from Setauket on Old Field Road, for Buffleheads in winter.

* **Old Field Point** (p. 94), at the end of Old Field Road, is the best local lookout for loons and eiders.

* **Mount Sinai Harbor** (p. 94), north of Mount Sinai, is a breeding area for Yellow-crowned Night Heron, Clapper Rail, Rough-winged and Bank Swallows.

* **Sweezy Pond Bogs,** southwest of Riverhead, south on Moriches Riverhead Road, has breeding Purple Martins.

* **Northville.** In autumn American Golden Plover and Water Pipit frequent the farm fields.

*** **Orient Point** (opposite), on the northern fluke of Long Island, made famous by 60 years of outstanding observations by Roy Latham. An excellent area for seabirds in winter; for the autumn migration from Rhode Island by way of Fisher's, Great Gull, and Plum Islands, bringing interesting rarities (Corn Crake recently). (1) The causeway on Route 25 east of East Marion is worth a search. Dan Pond, north of the causeway has Osprey, Marsh Hawk, herons, gulls, and terns in summer; Orient Harbor, south of the causeway, often has summering but nonbreeding loons, cormorants, and even White-winged Scoters; the marsh, east of causeway, has breeding species of Habitat M and S, including Clapper Rails. (2) The extreme end of Orient Point, 0.5 mile beyond end of Route 25, overlooks Plum Gut. Park car and walk 0.5 mile along beach. In winter, watch for both loons, grebes, flocks of Greater Scaup, Common Goldeneye, Oldsquaw, an occasional Harlequin Duck, Common and King Eiders, all three scoters, and Red-breasted Merganser. Search for Purple Sandpiper on the rocks and be alert for almost any species of gull. (3) In Orient Beach State Park, 500 feet west of the point, during winter look for flocks of Black Duck, Greater Scaup, Common Goldeneye, and Oldsquaw on the water; an occasional Snowy or Short-eared Owl on the meadows; Horned Larks on the beaches; and Snow Buntings at the parking field. In summer look for breeding Osprey, Piping Plover, Common and Least Terns (at extreme western end), and Horned Lark. (4) Two miles west of the point, turn south from Route 25 on Narrow River Road, which passes through marshland and meadows where Osprey nests. In winter look for Rough-legged, Marsh, and Sparrow Hawks, Snowy and Short-eared Owls, Horned Larks, Eastern Meadowlarks, Lapland Longspurs, and other Habitat U species. Return to Route 25 by Village Lane.

Along the south shore of the Suffolk County mainland are a series of inlets and creeks leading into Great South Bay; upstream are interesting ponds and woodlands.

* **Argyle Park,** in Babylon, is excellent in winter for a wide variety of waterfowl and wintering Fish Crows. Reached via Montauk Highway (Route 27A) to Argyle Road, Babylon.

* **Belmont Lake State Park** is north of Babylon, harbors waterfowl in winter: Shoveler, Gadwall, European Widgeon, Green-winged Teal, Ringed-necked Duck, Canvasback, Ruddy Duck, and Hooded Merganser.

Car: Entrance from Southern State Parkway, Exits 37 and 38.

** **Heckscher State Park** is in two sections: one south of Great River on Great South Bay; the other north of Great River on the west side of the Connetquot River. The park is varied, with dry oak woodland, marshes, fields, and waterfront. Interesting for landbird migration in autumn; good for Rough-legged Hawk, half-hardy landbirds, and waterfowl in winter.

Car: Entrances from Route 27 and 27A, Heckscher Spur to southern section.

** **Bayard Cutting Arboretum** is on the west side of the Connetquot

GREEN
HERON

River. Formerly a private estate, now open to the public. Towering ever-greens, marshy woodlands with azaleas and rhododendron, and broad lawns make it a "museum" of local breeding birds. A large colony of House Finches is located here. In winter, bird feeders at the houses hold a variety of small birds.

Car: Entrance from Route 27A just east of East Islip.

* **Lace Mill Pond** (Great Patchogue Lake), north of Patchogue, is fair for wintering ducks, with the same variety as Argyle Pond.

Car: State Route 27, south on State Route 112, west on Roe Boulevard.

** **Wertheim Preserve,** in South Haven south of the railroad tracks, at the mouth of the Carman's River. A tract of unspoiled beauty, with a lake. A hunting preserve, deeded to the Federal Government as a future wildlife refuge. In winter, flocks of Mallard, Black Duck, American Widgeon, Green-winged Teal, and American Coot. Also Rough-legged and Marsh Hawks. Bitterns and several species of rails are regular here. Seek permission to enter from the caretaker.

** **Suffolk Game Lodge,** north of South Haven on Carman's River, is a large shooting preserve with the river dammed to form a lake. The Bald Eagle has been known to winter here; and many species of ducks. The woods are stocked with Wild Turkey, Ruffed Grouse, Ring-necked Pheasant, and Hungarian Partridge. Seek permission to enter from the main lodge.

* **Quogue** (p. 90), on Quantuck Bay, is the waterfowl sanctuary of Southampton Township Wildfowl Association, roughly 1500 acres of wet-lands and water which include Upper Quantuck Bay and the ice pond to the north. Many species of waterfowl winter; several remain to breed. Hermit Thrush breeds here. Just west, a small pond on the Westhampton-Quogue boundary gives close-up views of Hooded Merganser in winter.

In the middle of the island large areas of pine-oak scrub remain, with such breeding species as the Red-tailed Hawk, Ruffed Grouse, Great Horned Owl, Whip-poor-will, Hermit Thrush, Blue-winged Warbler, Chestnut-sided Warbler, Pine Warbler, Prairie Warbler, and Grasshopper, Vesper, and Field Sparrows.

* **Manorville.** Grasshopper, Vesper, and Field Sparrows nest by the west-ern end of the fence on the south side of the Grumman Aircraft plant.

* **Calverton** is on the Peconic River. Vesper Sparrows breed and winter along Swan Pond Road, off Wading River Road.

* **Coram** is at the junction of Routes 25 and 112. The Hermit Thrush nests about 1 mile north on Route 112. Also at Speonk, Quogue, Manorville.

** **Hampton Bays** (p. 90). Route 27 approaching Hampton Bays from the west passes under a railroad bridge; about 0.5 mile beyond the bridge turn north toward Bellows Pond. Hermit Thrushes are heard singing at dusk from 0.5 to about 1 mile along the road in breeding season.

** **Roosevelt Estate,** in Sayville, is abandoned 30 acres on the south side of Route 27A, about 1 mile east of Sayville town and directly west of Lotus Lake. In spring, one of the finest landbird migration areas in southern Suffolk County.

* **Brookhaven,** on Mott Lane, on the west side of the road opposite an abandoned tree nursery, for Woodcock flights on moonlit nights in April. Long-eared Owls frequent this area in winter.

***ATLANTIC OCEAN:** Perhaps the most fascinating, and certainly the most unpredictable habitat for the local bird watcher, is the ocean itself. Fishing boats are available from Sheepshead Bay in Brooklyn, Atlantic Beach, Point Lookout, Freeport, Bayshore, Captree Island, Babylon, Shinnecock, Montauk, and other ports. Usually the farther east the better. The best seasons are late May through mid-June; late August through September. Pelagic bird watching is always best after three days of winds from the southwest, south, southeast, or east, except in winter, when a nor'easter is best, but ocean bird watching is unpredictable at all seasons. There are two types of boats. The first type — the party or "open" boat — is open to anyone until capacity is reached; they usually leave before 7:00 A.M., and go where the captain wants to. Boats fishing for flounder or other bottom fish will not go far offshore; those fishing for mackerel or bluefish may go 20–35 miles out, which is worthwhile. Rates for bluefish are about $12 per person per day. The second type — the charter boat, which must be engaged in advance — costs about $80 to $150 per day, and will go where the passengers wish. From Nassau County, the "Acid Grounds" and the "Mud Hole" are two popular productive areas. Birds may be attracted by "chumming" — spreading a trail of minced menhaden, or puffed cereals soaked in fish oil, on the water. Start early to attract gulls from the harbor, since a large gull "following" often brings in the pelagics. A recent Linnaean Society trip on a May 30 recorded all three shearwaters, all three jaegers, both petrels, phalaropes, rare gulls, and the state's first Yellow-nosed Albatross not far from Jones Inlet. The Sooty Shearwater is common in late May. Late summer is best for Wilson's Petrel, Cory's and Greater Shearwaters, and Pomarine Jaeger. Winter is the time for Gannet, Black-legged Kittiwake and other rare gulls, and alcids. Recommended: Seasickness pills and warm clothing with a waterproof outer covering and gloves at any season — the warmest possible in winter.

WESTCHESTER COUNTY: Directly north of the Bronx and bordered on the east by Long Island Sound and Connecticut, on the north by Putnam County, and on the west by the Hudson River. Migrants follow the Hudson

CANADA
GOOSE

River, the Sound shore, and the several ridgelines that run from northeast to southwest through the county. The open fields, high hills, and woodlands of the northern section have breeding birds perhaps equally of the Canadian and Transition Zones.

    * Long Island Sound. Thousands of ducks and geese winter in the bays and inlets. The most numerous species in order of abundance are: Greater Scaup, Black Duck, Canvasback, Common Goldeneye, Red-breasted Merganser, Canada Goose, Mallard, American Widgeon, Bufflehead, Old-squaw, and an occasional scoter, Ruddy Duck, or other species.

    Car: Directions to the best lookouts are from US Route 1; where roads are marked "Private," always seek permission. (1) Davenport Neck, New Rochelle. South on Echo Avenue, left on Hudson Parkway, right on Davenport to end. (2) Premium Point, New Rochelle–Larchmont. East on Premium Point Road to end, or east on Dillon, right on Pryer Manor Road to Pryer Lane. (3) Horseshoe Harbor, Larchmont. South on Larchmont Avenue to end. (4) Greacen Point, Mamaroneck. South on Orienta Avenue, right on Greacen Point Road to end. (5) Mamaroneck Harbor, Mamaroneck. South on Orienta Avenue to end, or south on Orienta Avenue and left on Seahaven Lane. (Great Cormorants and Purple Sandpipers at end of Larchmont jetty in winter.) (6) Van Amringe Mill Pond, on Brevoort Lane, for Hooded Mergansers in winter.

    ** Milton Harbor, Rye. The three following vantage points are open to the public in winter. (1) East from Route 1 on Oakland Beach Avenue, south on Hixon Street to golf course at end. Walk south for waterfowl, hawks, owls, and wintering finches; recent finds include Snowy Owl, Ruffed Grouse, and Broad-winged Hawk in December. (2) East from Route 1 on Oakland Beach Avenue, south on Stuyvesant Avenue to Milton Point, where car may be parked overlooking the bay. (3) East from Route 1 on Barlow Lane (just east of Mamaroneck-Rye line) to end.

*** **Playland Lake–Manursing Island,** Rye, an area of county parks, private clubs, and estates, extending from Oakland Beach, where Purple Sandpipers winter, to North Manursing Island, where Purple Martins nest. Between the two "Purples" are the best bird-watching habitats in the Sound shore area, with sandy beaches, shingle, and bluff, and behind them Playland Lake with its surrounding marshlands, meadows, woods, tidal flats, and bays.

Playland Lake is a rowboat lake in summer, but once the boats are hauled up after Labor Day the ducks return. On one October morning there were 12,000 Greater Scaup. Well into December, flocks of Canada Goose, Black Duck, Canvasback, Greater Scaup, Common Goldeneye, Bufflehead, three species of mergansers, and American Coot rest and feed here. Offshore more waterfowl are found — Horned Grebes, Oldsquaws, a few scoters, and an occasional Common Loon. In winter Great Blue Herons may be found along the shores of the islands in the lake. And the birch groves and thickets east of the lake shelter Mourning Doves, Robins, Hermit Thrushes, and Red-winged Blackbirds. Wintering sparrows and finches are often abundant.

In winter, look for Red-tailed, Rough-legged, and Marsh Hawks, and in spring Osprey. There are many Laughing Gulls spring and fall, Bonaparte's Gulls in spring, and, occasionally, a "white-winged" gull.

In spring and autumn the woodlands north and south of the lake, bordering Manursing Way, become a migration trap for flycatchers, thrushes, vireos, warblers, and other landbird migrants. Breeding birds include the Belted Kingfisher, Traill's Flycatcher, Carolina Wren, Veery, White-eyed Vireo, and the abundant House Finch. Manursing Way goes east from Forest Avenue, and by following it east to its end (where there are evergreen groves worth investigating in winter) and turning left to Kirby Lane one reaches another vantage point for waterfowl, herons, and shorebirds.

Car: From Route 1 go east on Playland Parkway to end, or from New England Thruway (Int. 95) exit at Rye to Playland Parkway. No park toll for bird watchers in off season (show binoculars); for Manursing Way, turn north from Playland Parkway on Forest Avenue (last traffic light before park entrance) for about 1 mile.

* **Rye City Park,** 25 acres. A woodland sanctuary with a resident biologist; sometimes interesting in migration. Resident Tufted Titmouse, Yellow-breasted Chat, Scarlet Tanager, Rose-breasted Grosbeak. US Route 1, Rye. Entrance, opposite Episcopal Church.

* **Saxon Woods Park,** Scarsdale-Harrison. Large, mostly wooded; surprisingly, never very fruitful.

Car: Hutchinson River Parkway to Exit 22 or 23.

* **Harrison.** There is a large tract of open meadows on West Street west of Union Avenue. American Woodcock give aerial courtship display on April evenings.

Car: Hutchinson River Parkway to Exit 23, east on Union Avenue, left on West Street.

* **Greenwood Union Cemetery,** North Street, Rye, is occasionally good in winter.

* **Maple Moor Golf Course,** Harrison, has woods along both sides of Hutchinson River Parkway. Worth searching for owls in winter.

Car: Exit from Hutchinson River Parkway at State Route 127 south, left on North Street.

* **Nature Study Woods** (p. 104), 1500 acres along Hutchinson River Parkway northwest of New Rochelle. A neglected wet woodland bordering a water-filled ditch at the south end of Long Lake of Hutchinson River. Of local interest for common breeding species; landbird migrants spring and fall.

Public transportation: From New Rochelle railroad station take blue bus, marked Disbrow Circle, up Webster Avenue to first woodland.

Car: Hutchinson River Parkway to Webster Avenue (Exit 11), south to first woods.

* **Tibbetts Brook Park,** Yonkers. Open only to residents of Westchester County. A mixed parkland with a brook flowing through a string of ponds from north to south, reportedly fair to good in migration.

Car: Saw Mill River Parkway, Exit 4A.

BARRED
OWL

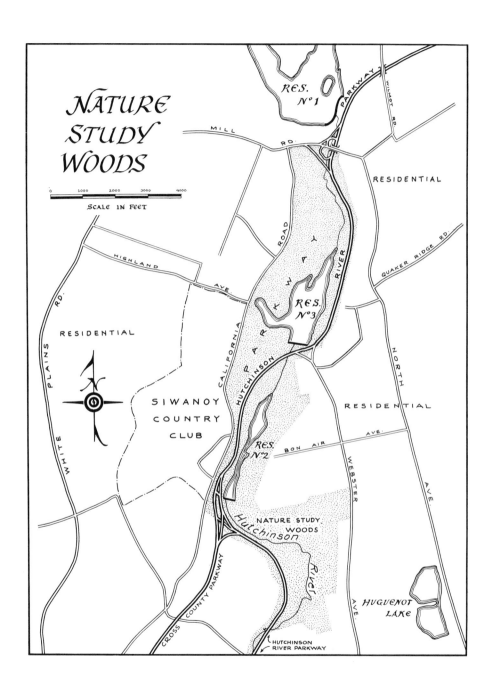

NATURE STUDY WOODS

SCALE IN FEET

0   1000   2000   3000   4000

RES. No 1

MILL RD.

PARKWAY

WILMOT RD.

RESIDENTIAL

HIGHLAND AVE.

PARKWAY ROAD

RIVER

QUAKER RIDGE RD.

RES. No 3

WHITE PLAINS RD.

RESIDENTIAL

N

SIWANOY COUNTRY CLUB

CALIFORNIA

HUTCHINSON PARK

NORTH AVE.

RESIDENTIAL

BON AIR AVE.

RES. No 2

AVE.

WEBSTER AVE.

NATURE STUDY WOODS

Hutchinson

CROSS COUNTY PARKWAY

River

AVE.

HUGUENOT LAKE

HUTCHINSON RIVER PARKWAY

** **Hillview Reservoir,** Yonkers, is east of the New York State Thruway. A resting and feeding site for waterfowl from autumn to spring; and a better-than-average place for rare "white-winged" gulls; surrounding conifers worth a search in winter.

Car: New York State Thruway Exit 1 to Central Park Avenue, north on Central Park Avenue, right on Hillview, left on Kimball Avenue, and left Kimball Terrace. Access road on south side.

* **White Plains Reservoir,** White Plains, has thick pine plantings.

Car: From State Route 22 (North Broadway) in White Plains north on Orchard Street.

* **Silver Lake Park,** White Plains, is a scenic, craggy woodland with lakes and meadowlands. Said to be "only fair" in spring migration, but this attractive oak, beech, and tulip woodland might be worthwhile in early morning hours. It might have breeding Pileated Woodpeckers.

Car: From Route 22 (North Broadway) north on Lake Street to entrance north of Battle Monument.

** **Tarrytown Reservoir,** crossed by Neperan Road in Tarrytown. The reservoir is excellent in spring, fall, and winter. The spruces and pines to the south recently attracted a Black-backed Three-toed Woodpecker. Worthwhile too is the brushy swamp area on the northwest. This entire area is good for herons, waterfowl, and owls; also Blue-gray Gnatcatcher, warblers, and Orchard Oriole.

Car: Right from US Route 9 on Neperan Road, or Exit 23 from Saw Mill River Parkway, west on County House Road, left on Neperan Road.

** **Grassy Sprain Ridge,** from Tuckahoe Avenue in Yonkers north to Elmsford. Excellent in spring migration, a former (?) breeding area for the Kentucky Warbler. Other breeding birds include the Broad-winged Hawk, Yellow-throated Vireo, Yellow-breasted Chat, Worm-eating Warbler, and other woodland species.

Car: New York Thruway Exit 6, west on Tuckahoe Avenue, north on Sprain Brook Road, and north on Sprain Road. Investigate the several good marshy "holes" along Sprain Road and the woodlands across the Thruway overpasses. From Sprain Road, turn east on Jackson Avenue. The Reservoir to the south may be reached from Jackson Avenue or from the golf course on the east shore, off northbound Sprain Brook Parkway. Grassy Sprain Reservoir is no longer natural, or attractive to birds. North of Jackson Avenue the woodlands along Grassy Sprain Brook and the brush-lands below the power lines are well pathed to Ardsley Road and beyond. A planned extension of Sprain Brook Parkway here may destroy the magnificent climax woodland to the north. Parallel to the power lines is the Catskill Aqueduct, a grassy track through open areas and woodlands. For a good mile-long section, turn east from State Route 9A or west from State Route

BROAD-WINGED
HAWKS

100A onto Payne Street, Elmsford. A dirt road, between Endicott and See Avenues, leads south to the aqueduct. Detailed local maps show the aqueduct.

** Eastview. The pasturelands east of Eastview and north of State Route 100C are excellent for Habitat U species. Search open fields in summer for Bobolinks and Grasshopper Sparrows. A good area for the migration of hawks, shrikes, swallows, warblers, and White-crowned Sparrows in various seasons. South of Route 100C a small reservoir attracts Bufflehead, herons, and sandpipers in season.

** Elmsford Ridge, at the intersection of Routes 100C and 9A, is one of the county's most famous warbler migration spots. The southwest quadrant south is best.

Hawthorne. There are at least three places of interest, all reached from Stevens Avenue, which runs from the Taconic State Parkway east to Columbus Avenue. (1) *Cedar Knolls, north of Stevens Avenue between Warren and Columbus Avenues, has a pasture with narrow wooded borders. The hilltop of this ridge is fine for the migration of hawks, nighthawks, swallows, and Bobolinks in late summer and autumn. In April, Snow Geese pass over and Woodcock perform after dark. Breeding species include Indigo Bunting, Bobolink, and Grasshopper Sparrow. Connecticut Warblers are more common here than elsewhere in autumn, especially along a trail between two pastures directly opposite Fox Hill Road. (2) ** "Frog Pond," north of Stevens Avenue about 300 yards west of Columbus Avenue. This is a rich bottomland alder swamp bounded by pastures, woodland, and wooded swamp. Noted for Virginia Rail, Sora, and all the Habitat F species, including Wood Duck, American Bittern, and Traill's Flycatcher. Lawrence's Warbler nested here in 1962; Eastern Bluebirds nest in the nearby orchard. Sixty-one species breed in this area. (3) * Dense pine and spruce plantation. Excellent for warbler flights; Boreal Chickadee wintered in 1961–62 and 1963–64; Barred and Long-eared Owls have been found here in winter. This is private property. Go north from Stevens Avenue on Warren Avenue, take the third right, turn the corner, and park at the first left turn.

Car: Right from Taconic State Parkway on Stevens Avenue. Or north from White Plains on State Route 22, left across Kensico Dam, then northward to the main road north (Columbus Avenue) for about a mile to Stevens Avenue.

*** **Croton Point Park** (p. 109), on the Hudson River. The best place inland for the Red-necked Grebe and Bald Eagle; a good place for owls, "white-winged" gulls, half-hardy landbirds, and waterfowl. For owls, work the evergreens on the southern slope of the Point; for eagles, the trees near the Point or the ice floes on the river; for hawks, the woodlands; for gulls, the garbage dump or fields near the park entrance. This park should be a fine vantage point for birds using the Hudson River flyway, but bird watchers seem to have neglected it during migration seasons.

Public transportation: New York Central Railroad to Harmon-on-Hudson Station, walk west on Croton Point Avenue.

Car: US Route 9, left on Croton Point Avenue to park.

* **George's Island County Park,** Montrose. May have eagles in winter, if Croton Point does not.

Car: Route 9 north to Montrose, west on Dutch Street to end.

* **Brinton Brook Sanctuary** (112 acres), Croton-on-Hudson. An attractive woodland with a small pond, maintained by the Saw Mill River Audubon Society. Excellent for landbirds spring and fall, interesting in winter.

Car: North from Croton-on-Hudson for about 2 miles, right at sign on right "Brinton-Kenoten, Private Drive," opposite a white picket fence.

* **Pleasantville.** (1) * Gate of Heaven Cemetery has American Widgeons all winter on its small pond, and a large Crow roost. North from Hawthorne

on Route 141. (2) * Flag Hill, an autumn hawk lookout and excellent bird watching in mixed cover spring and fall. West from Pleasantville on Ossining Road, right on Hardscrabble Road for 1.5 miles to steep, rocky road on right; park and walk to summit. (3) * Pocantico Lake Reservoir, in Briarcliff Manor, has Habitat F species that include American Bittern, rails, Common Gallinule; and good landbird flights in spring. West from Pleasantville on State Route 117, right on Old Sleepy Hollow Road for about 1 mile, right for 0.75 mile to lakeshore.

Car: Saw Mill River Parkway, Exit 28 to Pleasantville.

* **Amawalk Reservoir,** north-central Westchester. A rich hillside for Habitat W species, including Acadian Flycatchers on the southern side.

Car: Saw Mill River Parkway north to Katonah, west on State Route 35, right on Lake Road just before crossing the dam. Follow Lake Road along the eastern shore.

** **Ward Poundridge Reservation** (6 square miles), northeast of Bedford Village. The park comprises well-watered woodlands and upland fields, reaching an elevation of 870 feet. The increasing infiltration of Canadian Zone breeding species is evident here — including Red-breasted Nuthatch, Winter Wren, Blackburnian and Canada Warblers, and possibly Slate-colored Juncos. Here too are records of southern species such as the Turkey Vulture, Tufted Titmouse, Hooded Warbler, and Louisiana Water-thrush. Breeding birds include the Broad-winged Hawk, Ruffed Grouse, Barred Owl, Whip-poor-will, Cedar Waxwing, and other Habitat W birds. In the marshy meadows east of the entrance, Eastern Bluebirds, Bobolinks, and Grasshopper Sparrows breed. Some winters the evergreen groves are excellent for Evening and Pine Grosbeaks, Common Redpolls, Pine Siskins, and crossbills; other years these species forsake the park entirely.

Car: North on State Route 22 from Bedford Village, right on State Route 121 to the entrance 300 yards south of the village of Cross River.

Byram Lake area, south of Bedford Village. In this area there are three private sanctuaries. (1) * Westmoreland Sanctuary (107 acres) and (2) * Arthur W. Butler Memorial Sanctuary (225 acres) face each other on Chestnut Ridge Road. Westmoreland, open year round, has an interesting breeding-bird list — 10 pairs of Worm-eating Warblers in 1962 — and some of the more northern species as well. The Butler Sanctuary includes a 3-acre marsh and 30 acres of swampy woodland with typical Habitat F and W species.

Car: South from Bedford Village on Route 22, right on State Route 172 for about 2 miles, left on Chestnut Ridge Road.

(3) ** Mianus River Gorge Wildlife Refuge and Botanical Preserve, 1.25 miles along the Mianus River southeast of Bedford Village. Open April 1 to January 1. A narrow river valley of great scenic beauty, with ancient hem-

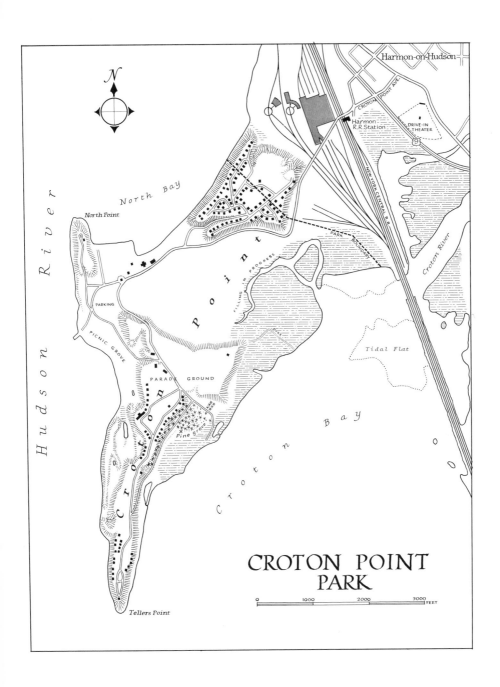

Harmon-on-Hudson

CROTON POINT AVE.

Harmon
R.R.Station

DRIVE-IN
THEATER

N

NEW YORK CENTRAL R.R.

Croton River

North Bay

North Point

PARK BOUNDARY

FILLING IN PROGRESS

C r o t o n   P o i n t

PARKING

PICNIC GROVE

Tidal Flat

PARADE GROUND

Pine Grove

C r o t o n   B a y

H u d s o n   R i v e r

C r o t o n

Tellers Point

CROTON POINT
PARK

0   1000   2000   3000 FEET

locks and mixed hardwoods. It has typical Habitat W breeding species —
Barred and Great Horned Owls, Louisiana Waterthrush, Worm-eating and
Black-throated Green Warblers.

Car: East from Route 22, Bedford Village, on Poundridge Road, for about
a mile, right on Long Ridge Road (Stanford Road) for 0.5 mile, right on
Millers Mill Road, and then directly left on Mianus River Road. Or from
Exit 31 on the Merritt Parkway, Greenwich, Connecticut: north on North
Street for 1.8 miles, right on North Stanwich Road for 1.7 miles, left on
Taconic Road for 1.3 miles, right on East Middle Patent Road for 2.2 miles,
right on Mianus River Road for 1.8 miles to entrance.

* **Peach Lake,** in the northeastern corner of the county, has the typical
varied habitat of this area. Breeding species include Cliff Swallow, Blackburnian and Golden-winged Warblers, Henslow's Sparrow, and possibly
Red-shouldered and Red-tailed Hawks, Acadian Flycatcher, and Warbling
Vireo.

Car: North from Bedford Village on State Route 22, right on State Route
121.

** **Blue Mountain Reservation** is across the county south of Peekskill.
It is largely wooded, with two small ponds — a typical Habitat W. The
summit of Blue Mountain (960 feet) is considered a good hawk lookout in
autumn when the weather is clear and the winds north to west.

Car: East from Route 9 in Peekskill on US Route 202, right on Maple
Avenue to Pleasantside, right on Montrose Station Road into Reservation.

PUTNAM COUNTY: North of Westchester, and similar to that county in bird
habitat. A small county without a single major town; a county of farms,
estates, large reservoirs, lakes, and rolling tree-clad hills, with Connecticut
on the east, the Hudson River on the west, and Dutchess County on the
north.

** **Constitution Island,** a peninsula that juts into the Hudson River south
of Cold Spring. It is a Federal Government reservation. Permission to enter
is obtained at the museum on the grounds. Heavily wooded, with much
wooded swampland where the Wood Duck breeds. The best landbird
migration spot in the county in spring; 80 species have been recorded on
one recent May day.

Car: West from State Route 9D in Cold Spring on State Route 301 as far
as possible, turn left and then make a series of turns to cross a bridge over
railroad tracks. Go south on the river side of the tracks about 200 yards,
park, and walk south along the tracks. West of the tracks is a large freshwater marsh with Habitat M breeding birds, including Virginia Rails. A
few linger into January, feeding along the creeklet beside the tracks. Birds
of prey and Pileated Woodpeckers occur the year round.

* **Manitou Swamp** is north of Bear Mountain Bridge. A narrow cattail marsh has Virginia Rails, birds of prey, and other Habitat F birds; herons in late summer; better-than-average variety in winter.

Car: North from Bear Mountain Bridge on Route 9D, left at the first available turn, park by the railroad station and walk north or south along the tracks.

* **Clarence Fahnestock Memorial Park** and **Roaring Brook Park** are along the Taconic State Parkway. These parks are true wilderness, largely forested, with a chain of lakes running north and south. The bird life is typical Habitat W, with the county's largest population of breeding birds of prey, Pileated Woodpecker, and Ruffed Grouse.

PILEATED
WOODPECKER

Car: Exit from Taconic Parkway at Stillwater Lake for southern section; on State Route 301 west for Canopus Pond in northwest.

* **West Branch Reservoir,** west of Carmel, for waterfowl in autumn and into winter. It is best at the south end and where the highway crosses.

Car: West from Carmel on Route 301.

* **Lake Mahopac,** between Mahopac Falls and Mahopac, for waterfowl in autumn and early winter.

Car: West from Mahopac on US Route 6, right on State Route 6N.

* **Oscawana Lake,** west of Taconic State Parkway, for ducks in autumn and early winter.

Car: West from Taconic Parkway on State Route 301 to Fahnestock Corners, south on unnumbered roads to Dennytown, east and south to Christian Corners, south to lake.

** Shrub Oak Memorial Park, northwest of Shrub Oak at the base of Piano Mountain. A second-growth woodland with a wooded swamp and lake. The landbird migration is good on the southern slope in spring. Blue-winged, Golden-winged, Brewster's, Hooded, and Worm-eating Warblers breed. About 100 yards west of lake, a trail starts leading to the summit of the mountain, an autumn lookout for hawks.

Car: North from Route 6 in Shrub Oak on Barger Road.

HOODED
WARBLER

** Mount Nimham, between Carmel and Kent Cliffs, is the highest point in Putnam County. Excellent in spring migration and for a long list of breeding species of Habitat U and W lists.

Car: Route 6 north to Carmel, west on State Route 301. Just across West Branch Reservoir causeway, take right fork (Gypsy Trail Road). At 2.4 miles, trail to summit starts on left.

* Patterson, south of Pawling. The "Great Swamp," wooded and cut by numerous creeks, runs north and east toward Pawling. Strangely, it has breeding birds with southern affinities, and is the first breeding location in the county for the Mockingbird and Blue-gray Gnatcatcher. Explore by canoe from State Route 311 just east of Patterson.

DUTCHESS COUNTY: North of Putnam, a county of rural and rolling aspect with ridges and valleys running northeast and southwest. The eastern third is more rugged, and some of the higher hills (to 2300 feet) are forested mostly with second-growth hardwoods and harbor Canadian Zone birds. Groves of big trees and landscaped grounds of large estates attract Habitat A species. The weather is warmer in summer and colder in winter than in the city and the impressive spring migration is usually one or two days later. Often, if bad weather intervenes, some waves are missed completely. Part of its migration may arrive from the southeast, across the river. Along the river are extensive marshes.

In the county one finds both southern and northern elements breeding. Among the southern species noteworthy for our region are the Turkey Vulture (Stissing Mountain, and Thompson Peak area), Blue-gray Gnatcatcher, Worm-eating Warbler, and Cerulean Warbler (Cruger's Island and Rhinebeck). Northern species include Brown Creeper (fairly common, northern half), Hermit Thrush, Winter Wren, Solitary Vireo, Black-throated Blue, Nashville, and Canada Warblers and Slate-colored Junco (all on Brace Mountain). Other interesting breeders include Great Blue Heron (Tamarack Swamp).

* Vassar College Campus, Poughkeepsie, is a landscaped campus with golf course, small lake, and stream. Summer residents include Wood Duck, Red-tailed Hawk, both cuckoos, Barred Owl, Common Nighthawk, Pileated Woodpecker, Bobolink, and Warbling Vireo.

Car: East from US Route 9 on Main Street, north on North Clinton to Campus. The lake is on Creek Road east of the campus.

Pine Plains, in northern part of county. (1) Three ponds — Thompson Pond, Stissing Lake, and Mud Pond — south of village. ** Thompson Pond, the property of the Nature Conservancy, is 0.5 mile long and fringed with marshy wooded swamps, old pastures, and woodlands. There is an old road along the western side of the pond, and a trail on the eastern side. (2) * Stissing Mountain (1400 feet), west of ponds, is forested with hardwoods, white pine, and hemlock. Breeding birds include: Turkey Vulture, American Woodcock, Great Horned Owl, Whip-poor-will (some years), Traill's Flycatcher, Purple Martin, Hermit Thrush (southern end of the mountain), and Worm-eating Warbler (on Lake Road at foot of the mountain). Golden-winged and Blue-winged Warblers nest along Lake Road north of Thompson Pond; Black-throated Green Warbler at foot of the mountain; and the Louisiana Waterthrush by a stream at the southwestern corner of Thompson Pond. (3) Fields along State Route 199 west of Pine Plains have Bobolink and Grasshopper, Savannah, and Vesper Sparrows. (4) Briarcliffe Farm, a cattle ranch almost devoid of vegetation, borders Thompson Pond to south, and has wintering waterfowl. Ask permission to enter at the office on State Route 82A. Ducks winter on Halcyon Pond (or Buttermilk Pond) south of Briarcliffe Lane; look for shorebirds in August and September.

Car: Lake Road from Pine Plains.

* Innisfree Gardens (600 acres), between Washington Hollow and Millbrook. Maintained by a foundation, open to the public in summer for a small fee. Habitats include oriental gardens, hemlock groves, second-growth woodland, and Tyrell Lake. Nesting species include Blue-gray Gnatcatcher, Blackburnian Warbler, and Eastern Bluebird.

Car: South from US Route 44, just east of Washington Hollow, on Tyrell Road; or east from Taconic State Parkway, 4 miles north of State Route 55 intersection, on Tyrell Road.

** **Mount Rutsen,** northwest of Rhinebeck, is a small hill with second-growth woodlands with wooded swamp. Cerulean Warblers breed at the intersection of the Mount Rutsen road and River Road.

Car: North from Rhinebeck on US Route 9, west on road to Mount Rutsen.

*** **Cruger's Island,** on the Hudson north of Rhinebeck, connected to the mainland by road, with large bays — mostly marsh — north and south. Along the road and on the island is the area's largest concentration of Cerulean Warblers. Also breeding: Least Bittern in north bay, Virginia Rail, both cuckoos, Traill's Flycatcher, Brown Creeper, Long-billed Marsh Wren, Blue-gray Gnatcatcher, and several warblers. A good area for migrating waterfowl in April, and Bald Eagles from late February to early March.

Car: North on State Route 9G from the intersection of US Route 9 and State Route 9G, north of Rhinebeck, for about 3 miles, left at the sign "Whaleback Inn." The road to the island is impassable in spring; park at sheds on right near entrance and walk.

Beacon, on the Hudson. (1) ** Mount Beacon, a fine hawk lookout in September and October when the wind is west to north. There is an inclined railway from State Route 9D in South Beacon to the top. A better lookout is from the fire tower a mile from the upper terminal. (2) * Beacon Dump, at the foot of Main Street in Beacon, has gulls in February, especially the "white-winged" gulls.

** **Tamarack Swamp,** in the northeastern corner of the county, features a pond with standing dead trees. Perhaps the New York area's only breeding Great Blue Herons. Northern Waterthrushes may nest here too.

Car: North from Taconic State Parkway on State Route 82A, right on the Shunpike (Route 57), left on Shurman Road for about 1 mile, keeping right, until it crosses the upper end of a pond. Private property; seek permission to enter.

** **Brace Mountain,** north of Salisbury, Connecticut, is the highest point in the county, and forest-covered.

Car: North from US Route 44 at the water fountain in Salisbury, Connecticut, for 7 miles on Mountain Road. The entrance to the trail is marked on the left just before the trail, on right, leads to Monument Mountain. An easy climb — 2 to 3 miles.

* **Turkey Hollow,** in Lithgow east of Millbrook. A deep glen with a stand of hemlock above a trout stream. Breeding species include Canada Warbler, Louisiana Waterthrush, Black-throated Green Warbler, Slate-colored Junco. Private property; seek permission to enter.

Car: East from Taconic State Parkway on US Route 44 through Millbrook to Lithgow. From a picnic area on the right a road leads to the house, where permission to enter the hollow may or may not be granted. Deep Hollow Road, between Lithgow and State Route 22 in Wassic, is very similar. Birding here should be confined to roadsides.

CANADA
WARBLER

ROCKLAND COUNTY (p. 116): A triangle on the west bank of the Hudson River north of New Jersey. Perhaps our least populated, most wooded, and most rural suburban county, but with houses, factories, and shopping centers fast replacing the farms, orchards, and woodlands of this rolling, hilly land. Its location on the river and its hilltops reaching to 1240 feet make spring migration spectacular. There are four main areas: (1) the Hudson shore with the Palisades, (2) the Hackensack Valley, parallel to the river but about 3 miles west, (3) the rolling farm country to the west, (4) the forested ridges and mountains along the northern and western borders.

All directions are given from US Route 9W, which follows the river from the southern to northern boundary.

** Tallman Mountains, a section of Palisades Interstate Park, just north of the New Jersey line. An area of mixed hardwoods above and below the Palisades, and a fine observation point for spring landbird migration; look for Virginia Rails, Soras, and passerines in the freshwater marshes along the shore.

Public transportation: Piermont Avenue bus south from Nyack.

Car: East from Route 9W at park entrance north of Palisades village.

* Piermont Pier, on the river in Piermont. Private but access permitted. This is a winter lookout for grebes, waterfowl, gulls, and possibly Bald Eagles. It has provided some of the county's records of shorebirds and marsh birds in all seasons.

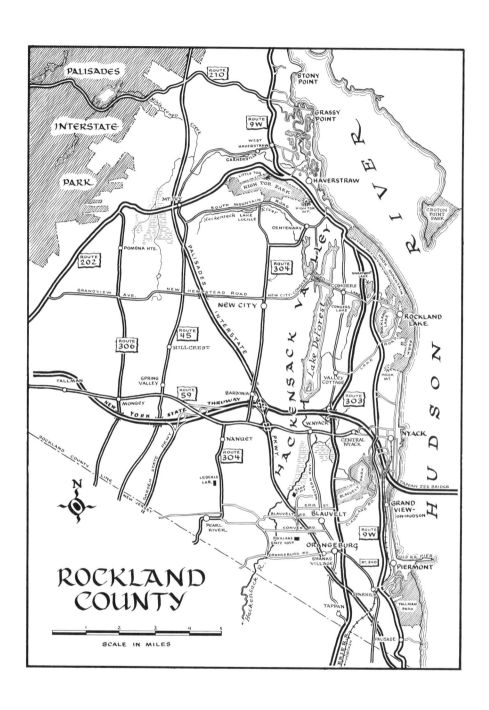

ROCKLAND
COUNTY

SCALE IN MILES

* **Blauvelt Section** of Palisades Interstate Park is interesting at all seasons. The area includes: (1) Tweed Boulevard, along the ridge from Nyack to Piermont; (2) Bradley Road, from South Nyack to Blauvelt village; (3) Clausland (Mountain) Road, northeast from State Route 303; and (4) Camp Bluefields, an old parade ground with fine brushlands and neglected pine plantations that attract northern finches in winter. Excellent for migrants.

Car: West from Route 9W about 2 miles north of Piermont. Campground best reached from the intersection of State Route 303 and Old Greenbush Road where a bar across a road uphill has a "No Parking" sign.

* **Friel Road,** southwest of Rockland State Hospital, has upland areas with broad fields and meadows with Habitat U species, particularly in migration. Look for Pileated Woodpeckers in the nearby woodlands.

* **Upper Nyack.** Hook Mountain Beach to Haverstraw, a shore walk once excellent for waterfowl, now fair; once a prime spot for eagles, now not. Still the best local area for the Carolina Wren.

Car: West from Route 9W to Nyack, north on river road to Upper Nyack.

* **Rockland Lake,** in Hook Mountain State Park between Route 9W and Rockland Lake village, has migrant waterfowl in spring and fall.

Car: East on Rockland Lake Road from Route 9W.

* **Congers Lake Road,** west of Rockland Lake, passes Swartwout Lake, Congers Lake, and Lake DeForest. All are waterfowl gathering spots and the roads around DeForest are still profitable landbird areas. Mockingbird breeds here, especially around the northern end (Ridge Road).

Car: West from Route 9W about 3 miles north of Nyack.

** **Little Tor,** Garnerville. Excellent for autumn hawk migration; good in spring for warblers and other landbirds. An outlook parking area, just below the summit, gives a panorama southward; a trail from the summit leads east about a mile, with excellent hawk-view points under the power lines and from the highest summit.

Car: West from Route 9W, at Haverstraw, on US Route 202, south on Central Highway, an inconspicuous paved road about 0.5 mile beyond the Low Tor Skating Rink and Garnerville School.

* **Haverstraw** to **Stony Point,** along the river. The marshes, ponds, and wooded strips are good for spring and fall migrants.

Car: Road along the river north from Haverstraw.

** **Stony Point Park,** a peninsula jutting into the river, is north of Stony Point. In winter, owls frequent the conifer groves, concentrations of Canvasbacks and other waterfowl are found on the river, and in former years the Bald Eagle was regular here. This is directly opposite George's Island County Park in Westchester County, a recent vantage point for eagles.

Car: East from Route 9W just north of Stony Point village.

** **Iona Island** is in the river at the entrance to Bear Mountain State Park. There are brackish marshes here where Least Bittern, Virginia Rail, possibly Sora, and Long-billed Marsh Wren nest. Look for cormorants and herons, gulls and terns in summer and fall; Rough-legged Hawk and waterfowl in winter.

Car: East from Route 9W, 2 miles south of entrance to Bear Mountain State Park.

*** **Bear Mountain-Harriman State Park** (42,000 acres), on the Rockland-Orange County line boundary, is an extensive natural area with second-growth hardwood forests, rhododendron bogs, and spring-fed lakes, productive in any season. In summer Broad-winged Hawks, Turkey Vultures, Pileated Woodpeckers, and warblers such as the Black-throated Green, Black-throated Blue, Blackburnian, Canada, Hooded, Worm-eating, and Louisiana Waterthrush breed.

BLACK-THROATED
GREEN WARBLER

At park headquarters across a pedestrian bridge east of Bear Mountain Inn are a trailside museum, zoo, and a nature trail; also maps showing hiking trails and the latest information on birds. Seven Lakes Drive, westward from Bear Mountain Inn: (1) passes Memorial Drive to the summit of Bear Mountain (1306 feet), an excellent hawk lookout in autumn; (2) rambles through beautiful woodland and beside shining lakes, passing down the west side of Lake Tiorati, a waterfowl resting area in late autumn;

(3) crosses State Route 210, and continues south as Stony Brook Drive to join State Route 17 just north of Sloatsburg in the Ramapo Mountain section. Ramapo, a village on Route 17, about 2 miles southeast of Sloatsburg, is 2 miles south of Ramapo Torne (1120 feet), the highest hill in a largely unexplored area.

ORANGE COUNTY: North and west of Rockland, shares some of its state parks, and is convenient to New York City by the New York Thruway. Primarily rural but developing rapidly, with industrial development mainly along the Hudson River. The northeast-southwest ridges are excellent for hawk flights, and for the spring migration of landbirds; the county boasts an excellent list of Habitat A, B, F, U, and W breeding species.

  *** **West Point Military Reservation,** on the Hudson River in the southeastern corner of the county. The Mine Road (Forest of Dean Road), twisting and narrow but paved, is open to the public, and crosses the reservation from Route 9W at Fort Montgomery on the east to State Route 293 on the west. Important stops are: (1) Long Mountain Trail. About 0.5 mile beyond Bear Mountain, where the road turns north, the Long Mountain Trail crosses Mine Road and goes westward to Weyant's Pond. A walk to this pond is probably the most productive in the area for the variety of birds in a short time. It winds through fields and woodlands, crosses (2) Popolopen Creek over a bridge, an excellent vantage point for marsh birds and Bank Swallow nesting in an exposed sandbank. The trail crosses (3) an old mine road (take a short walk on it in either direction and look for Blue-gray Gnatcatcher) and eventually reaches Weyant's Pond. Along Mine Road beyond the trail crossing, watch for Golden-winged Warblers and perhaps a hybrid warbler. Mine Road passes farms, overgrown with alder, willow, and birch, where nest White-eyed Vireo, Yellow-breasted Chat, Indigo Bunting, American Goldfinch, and where one hears American Woodcock in April. In winter, look for Pine Siskins and Common Redpolls

COMMON
REDPOLL

in the birches. Farther north are steep-walled, wooded slopes with Habitat W breeding species, including Red-tailed, Red-shouldered, and Broad-winged Hawks, Ruffed Grouse, and Pileated Woodpecker. (4) It passes along the north shore of Stillwell Lake, where loons and migrant waterfowl occur and possibly a Bald Eagle in winter.

Car: West from Route 9W, just north of Bear Mountain Circle at Fort Montgomery, on Mine Road (Forest of Dean Road), north on State Route 293 to Route 9W.

** **Storm King Mountain,** 3 miles south of the center of Cornwall-on-the-Hudson. A good lookout for hawks and geese in autumn, especially in October. A well-marked but steep trail starts opposite Storm King Arms Restaurant on Old Storm King Highway (State Route 218), and goes 0.75 mile to the overlook above river.

** **Mount Peter** has two lookouts near the highest point on State Route 17A between Greenwood Lake and Warwick. (1) Directly behind the Valley View Inn. (2) "Falcon Ridge," about 1 mile north of Route 17A. It is reached by the Appalachian Trail, which crosses Route 17A just east of the inn. From this ridge in one season, watchers have counted as many as 4000 hawks of 12 species, mostly Broad-wings.

** **Basher Kill** (about 6 square miles) is southeast of Monticello. The county's most extensive swamp, crossed by a deserted railroad bed. It is best in spring for migratory waterfowl, Osprey, warblers (in May), and Habitat M birds — bitterns, herons, and rails. On one May morning, 26 species of warblers (Cerulean included) were observed here.

COMMON
GALLINULE

Car: South from Route 17 at the Wurtzboro exit on US Route 209 for about 1 mile, left on the first paved road, which leads to the deserted roadbed. Park and walk several miles with the marsh on both sides.

** **Blooming Grove** is in the central part of the county. Along Ridge Road and adjacent Purgatory Road, Red-headed Woodpeckers are permanent residents; Cliff Swallows nest here, and Bobolinks breed in fields that in winter are likely locations for Rough-legged Hawks, Horned Larks, Eastern Meadowlarks, and Snow Buntings.

* **Tomahawk Lake,** to the west, is a waterfowl haven, best viewed from the dam at the southern end.

Car: North from State Route 17M at Chester on State Route 94 to Craigsville, left, and then a right fork on Hulsetown Road for 1.5 miles, left on Goshen Road for 1 mile, right on Ridge Road. For Tomahawk Lake: North from Craigsville on Hulsetown Road for about 0.75 mile, right to south end of lake.

ULSTER COUNTY: North of Orange County. Although it may be questionable to consider it part of Greater New York, it is as close to Times Square as Montauk Point. One pure Canadian Zone breeding habitat is mentioned here.

*** **Slide Mountain** (4204 feet) is the highest in the Catskills. There are mixed hardwoods on the lower slopes, mingled with conifers above; but there is no treeline. A breeding area for Canadian Zone species typical of more northern forests. Breeding species include the Ruffed Grouse, Pileated Woodpecker, Yellow-bellied Sapsucker, Yellow-bellied Flycatcher, both nuthatches, and all the thrushes, except the Wood, including *bicknelli* (above 3300 feet), the small race of the Gray-cheeked. Warblers are Parula, Black-throated Blue, Myrtle, Black-throated Green, Blackburnian, Blackpoll, Mourning, Canada, and other commoner species. Near the summit nest the Winter Wren, Slate-colored Junco, and White-throated Sparrow. Slide is easy to climb, on well-marked trails; there is a leanto at the summit.

Car: West from the New York Thruway, Kingston Exit E19, on State Route 28 to Big Indian, south on Oliverea Road for 12 miles to Winisook Lodge. The trail begins at the lodge.

CONNECTICUT: Since Connecticut may eventually have its own book, only one (nearby) area is mentioned here.

** **Audubon Center of Greenwich** (430 acres), North Greenwich. A varied habitat — upland fields, mixed-hardwood forest, a small lake with an alder swamp — offers rural bird finding at all seasons. There are carefully marked trails and a museum at headquarters for information on what is currently being seen. The bird list is similar to that for Mianus River Gorge.

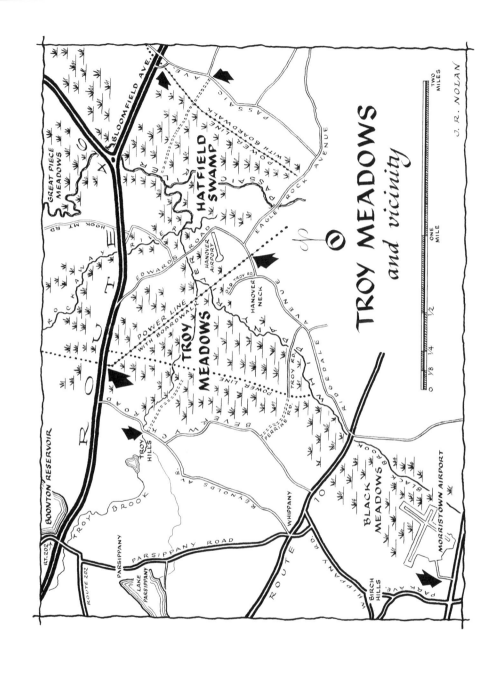

TROY MEADOWS *and vicinity*

J. R. NOLAN

Car: North from Merritt Parkway (State Route 15) at Exit 28 on Round Hill Road, left on Johns Street to Riversville Road and entrance.

NEW JERSEY: New York City bird watchers often ignore state lines and extend their operations into New Jersey as far as Cape May and the Delaware River. However, only a few places close to New York and of extraordinary interest are mentioned here.

*** **Troy Meadows** (opposite), northeast of Morristown between US Route 46 and State Route 10. It is a justly famous freshwater marsh — several square miles of waterway-laced meadow, marsh, and flooded woodlands, with hardwood groves on the higher ground. Though gradually losing to development, it is still our most extensive freshwater marsh with four sections: Troy Meadows, Hatfield Swamp, Black Meadows, and Great Piece Meadows. Hatfield Swamp and Troy Meadows are cut by power lines, under which are boardwalks that bird watchers may use. In Troy Meadows one may see or hear in early May such Habitat F species as the Pied-billed Grebe, Wood Duck, American and Least Bitterns, Virginia Rail (possibly the King Rail, Sora, Common Gallinule, Long-billed Marsh Wren, Swamp Sparrow, and several species of waterfowl. Watch for Yellow-breasted Chat at the southern end. A list of 100 species in one May day is quite possible.

Entrance: Boardwalk south from US Route 46, just west of Pine Brook (where power line crosses), and from the boardwalk at Ridgedale Avenue. A dirt road wanders into the marsh (from Beverwyck Road), and an island near the end is good for warblers. Canoeists may launch their craft where Edwards Road crosses the Whippany River.

** **Hatfield Swamp,** east of Troy Meadows. Good for wintering species such as the Brown Thrasher and Red-winged Blackbird. The alder thickets swarm with warblers in spring. Also, look for the Least Bittern, Blue-winged Teal, Ruddy Duck, and Common Gallinule. Traill's Flycatcher, White-eyed Vireo, and Sharp-tailed Sparrow nest here. Shorebirds, like the American Golden Plover, and the larger southern terns visit this swamp in autumn.

Entrance: Boardwalk from Bloomfield Avenue to Eagle Rock Avenue.

** **Black Meadows,** north of Morristown Airport. A good location for shrikes, Horned Larks, Lapland Longspurs, and Snow Buntings in winter. Good too for Rough-legged and other hawks in the adjacent marsh. Best watched from the airport north of State Route 510.

*** **Hackensack River,** has extensive tidal pools, mud flats, and salt marsh — a fine area for shorebirds, marsh birds, and water birds in proper seasons.

Car: (1) West from Holland Tunnel on US Route 1, right on State Route 506 (Belleville Turnpike) to where it passes under New Jersey Turnpike viaduct. Just south of this, the intersection of a dirt road cuts north, winds directly under the viaduct for about 0.5 mile to a spot where railroad tracks approach the viaduct. A remote spot, not recommended for an unaccompanied woman. (2) West from Lincoln Tunnel on State Route 3, south on State Route 17, left on Kingsland Avenue, right on Schuyler Avenue past the first traffic light to a bumpy dirt road on the left. The road goes into marsh past the North Arlington town dump, between two excellent pools, and dead-ends at the river. Other hazardous dirt roads transect the marsh in various directions; one joining with the Belleville Turnpike approach.

** **First Watchung Mountain,** in Upper Montclair. The site of an annual three-week cooperative hawk watch conducted by the Montclair Bird Club since 1957. The average for the past seven years: 4476, mostly Broad-wings. Numerous other species will be seen in migration.

Car: West from Lincoln Tunnel on State Route 3; south at the first exit after the junction of Routes 3 and 46 on Valley Road, right at Upper Montclair on Bellevue Avenue, right on Upper Mountain Avenue, left on Bradford Avenue for two blocks, right on Edgecliffe Road. Go to the top of the hill and 0.25 mile beyond rock quarry to a parking space at the corner of Crestmont Road. Walk east up a gentle slope on the southern side to top of the hill.

A BIRD WATCHER'S CALENDAR FOR
NEW YORK CITY AND VICINITY

JANUARY

The coldest month, but an exciting one. Large numbers of water birds linger in open bays and ocean. Try Montauk and eastern Long Island for Great Cormorant, eiders, Harlequin Duck, alcids, and the rarer gulls. Search beaches, marshlands, and dunes for Snowy Owl, Rough-legged Hawk, Purple Sandpiper, and the elusive Ipswich Sparrow. There may be northern finches — siskins, redpolls, grosbeaks, crossbills — in parks or woodlands. Look for Horned Lark, Snow Bunting, and the rarer Lapland Longspur in grassy areas. New York Harbor may have a rare gull. Bird feeders and sheltered thickets should be attractive to a lingering half-hardy bird or two.

FEBRUARY

Normally cold, with snow, and little change in bird activity. Keep your feeders filled. Few half-hardy birds will remain. With favorable weather, the end of the month will bring the vanguard of spring migrants — Red-winged Blackbird, Common Grackle, Brown-headed Cowbird — perhaps even Robin, Killdeer, and Marsh Hawk. Flocks of Canada Geese in the Mecox Bay area will increase, and some waterfowl will begin courtship activities.

MARCH

Often a month of hope denied — and wintry throughout; but normally March sees a definite quickening of activity, with a buildup of blackbird and Robin numbers, and a thinning of some winter visitants such as Horned Lark (although our breeding race will be feeding young), Tree Sparrow, and Snow Bunting. During midmonth, Gannets may move past our beaches and river ducks will increase in numbers. Among the incoming migrants: Black-crowned Night Heron, Belted Kingfisher, Fish Crow, Mourning Dove, Yellow-shafted Flicker, and Eastern Phoebe. By month's end the morning bird chorus will be definitely springlike. Now is a good time to check, repair, and set out your birdhouses.

APRIL

The migration swells in volume and variety, with new arrivals (and departures of wintering birds) marking every warm front. Central, Bronx, Van Cortlandt, and Brooklyn's Prospect Parks become showcases for the latest arrivals, and every city square and suburban garden will reflect the ever-changing spectacle. Waterfowl will reach their peak and dwindle, and along the beaches the first shorebirds will appear, often after bad weather. April brings herons and rails to the marshes, Laughing and rarer gulls to rivers and harbors, hawks along the hills, and swallows to sheltered waters. By month's end the first waves of wrens, kinglets, warblers, thrushes, and sparrows will have arrived. Look for birds wherever vegetation is advanced — along slopes with morning sun, beside sheltered streams, around ponds and marshes, especially on warm, windless days, even in light rain.

MAY

The month the bird watcher dreams about all year. Migration reaches its spectacular peak with birds in full song and nuptial plumage. Every day brings changes, and on "wave" days 30 or more new species may arrive. Get up and get out early! Parks, woodlands, and suburban gardens will have flycatchers, thrushes, warblers, vireos, tanagers, and other songbirds from ground level to the tops of the tallest oaks. Terns and skimmers will return to the beaches; the shorebird migration will be at its height about May 15. Watch weather charts for warm fronts with south winds, but occluded fronts may also dam the migration in our area. A long day in the field visiting many habitats on "the big day" may log 150 or more species. The migration wanes after May 21. At month's end, nesting has begun for many resident species, but offshore the pelagic migration is at its peak.

JUNE

Migration will end by June 7, and all breeding birds except American Goldfinches will be busily engaged in nesting. Song decreases during June, and by the end of the month is largely confined to early morning and evening. Many broods of young birds will be out of the nest. (Leave nestlings found on the ground undisturbed: the parents are usually nearby to take care of them.) Active, noisy colonies of terns, gulls, and skimmers now extend along the beaches. Drive slowly through them and do not intrude on foot. Cedar Waxwings, in our northern counties, begin nesting before the month is over.

JULY

The month when young birds take wing. You may see juveniles in their first complete plumage sharing the bird bath or feeder with their parents. Many species raise a second brood during July, particularly if the first nesting has failed. In midmonth the southward fall migration begins, with the arrival of flocks of shorebirds to mud flats and tidal shores. Late in July many songbird species stop singing and begin their fall molt. Ponds and reservoirs are dotted with broods of half-grown ducklings. Oceans and bays may have a summering loon, scoter, or some other nonbreeding species.

AUGUST

Normally our wettest, second-warmest month, with shorebird migration reaching its peak toward the end. Beaches, tidal pools, mud flats, and the edges of marine waterways will throng with terns, gulls, skimmers, shorebirds, and herons. Post-breeding wanderers, such as "southern" herons, Caspian and Forster's Terns, Parasitic Jaeger, and even rarer species may be present. Most waterfowl are in deep "eclipse" molt and consequently flightless. Songbirds are silent now, since they are either molting or occupied with a few late broods. Swallows begin flocking over fields and beaches, and through the woodlands and parks will move the vanguard of a silent, elusive landbird migration — the participants now in their dull, confusing winter dress. By month's end migration will reach full flood.

SEPTEMBER

For many watchers our most challenging month — a time for the unexpected. Fall migration crests to its peak everywhere, with September 15 a good average date for a high count of species. The bird life of the littoral reaches a climax, with swallows swarming overhead and shorebirds, gulls, terns, and other water birds in abundance. Bird watchers will look for tropical storms to bring southern exotics — perhaps a Sooty Tern, Brown Pelican, or other rarity. But cool fronts and northwest winds will spur landbird migration; then flycatchers, vireos, warblers, blackbirds, and sparrows may flood into woods and gardens. They may "pile up" in plantings along the southern strip of beaches, and with them you may find an unexpected vagrant from the Midwest or West such as a Western Flycatcher, Lark Sparrow, or Clay-colored Sparrow.

OCTOBER

This month brings cooler days and clear skies, and usually the first frost. The bird picture changes completely. Now the swallows, shorebirds, and herons are largely gone, and in their place come loons, cormorants, and flocks of waterfowl returning from the North. The southward hawk flight reaches its peak, with hawks over the ridges, and falcons, Osprey, and Marsh Hawk working along the beaches. This is the month for jays, flickers, late warblers, thrushes, and sparrows. Blackbirds gather in huge roosts, preparing to depart. There should be rarities, possibly a Western Tanager or a Yellow-headed Blackbird. Start keeping your feeders well stocked after the first frost.

NOVEMBER

The bird population thins with every new cold wave, but enough late-lingering migrants of many species will be present to make this a rewarding month. Offshore, loons are at their peak numbers and on ponds and bays the waterfowl flocks reach maximum size, increasing throughout the month until reduced by freezing waters and decimation by hunting. Flocks of wintering songbirds increase: now Black-capped Chickadee, Slate-colored Junco, White-throated Sparrow, and Tree Sparrow come to the well-stocked feeder. If this is to be a year of winter-finch invasions, you will soon be seeing crossbills, Evening Grosbeak, Pine Siskin, and so on, because this is the month for them to arrive.

DECEMBER

The southward migration (except for waterfowl) will end early in the month. The birds that linger will probably stay throughout the winter — if they survive. Waterfront areas, sheltered thickets, marshy streambanks, dense ornamental plantings, and garden feeders are now your most productive areas for bird watching. Although birds seem scarce in December, the annual Christmas Count taken by various local groups late in the month normally reveals 150 or more species in New York City and vicinity, regardless of the weather. From now on, particularly when snow covers the ground, feeders should be well stocked with mixed seed, sunflower seed, suet, gravel, and (if possible) drinking water.

CHECKLIST AND CALENDAR GRAPH

PRESENTED in the ensuing pages is a Checklist and Calendar Graph showing the species of birds that one may expect in the vicinity of New York City, including Long Island, during each of the twelve months.

The checklist itself is in the left-hand column. Here are given the 300 species that one is most likely to see at some time of the year in the New York City region. Some of these species are rare, irregular, or very local, and some are hard to find, so it is unlikely that you will list all these species in any one year. The total number of species recorded in the New York City area is more than 400 species, including several now extinct. By visiting a variety of habitats in the right seasons a diligent bird watcher should record from 240 to 275 species during an average year. The record for an individual bird watcher is said to be 303.

The Calendar Graph occupies the 12 right-hand columns. This indicates the period or periods of the year when a species is most likely to be found, and its relative abundance. Each solid line shows a period when the species is expected to be fairly common or regular somewhere in the area. Each dotted line shows the period when the species is uncommon, irregular, or rare. The graph does not include extreme dates of each species or all records of occurrence for each species. From this graph you can, by noting when a line begins or ends, determine (1) when a migrant first arrives in spring, (2) when it is at its commonest during migration, (3) whether it breeds in the area, (4) whether it is a scattered, uncommon breeding bird, (5) when the spring migration begins to taper off, (6) when it ends, if a nonbreeder, (7) when the first fall arrivals may appear, (8) when the bird is commonest in fall, (9) when the migration thins in fall, and (10) when it ends. You can also determine the approximate arrival dates, periods of maximum abundance, and departure dates of winter visitants. When you discover a bird well outside the period indicated, you can consider its appearance unusual, and worth reporting to the regional editors of *Audubon Field Notes* or *The Kingbird* (see page 158).

Between the Checklist on the left and the Calender Graph is a column entitled "Habitat." Here are indicated by symbols the habitat or habitats in which the species is most likely to be found (for the meaning of the symbols, see below, "Key to Habitats"). Since birds have wings and are subject to winds and weather and their own inclinations, no habitat key can be all-inclusive. Some species, like the Seaside Sparrow, the Wilson's Petrel, the Purple Sandpiper, and the Red Crossbill, are confined to one habitat, but many species will range widely at different seasons. Birds such as warblers, tanagers, and thrushes, which predominate in woodlands in spring, are abundant in shrubbery and low vegetation along the coastal strip in the fall. While you may expect to find seabirds only at sea, adverse weather conditions may force seabirds inland even to reservoirs and big rivers. The graph will help you know what to expect *where* and *when*.

Make a habit of keeping notes and lists and comparing your own observations with the accompanying chart. You will find that better birding will result from a knowledge of the birds to be expected in a given area at a given time of year. Submit, to those who keep records for your area, your reports of arrival and departure dates, based on your notes. Watch for the unusual and write up your observations in your notebook. If your observation seems unusual or remarkable in any way, make every effort to show the bird to experienced observers in your neighborhood; record keepers demand verification whenever possible.

The discovery of a rare bird, or of a common bird at an unusual time or place, is not only one of the rewards of bird watching but may be worthy of publication in an ornithological journal. The science of ornithology benefits immeasurably through the contributions of bird watchers.

KEY TO HABITATS

A   Average landscaped areas, gardens, parks, orchards, woodland edges, feeders

B   Brushy fields, beach shrubbery, thickets

C   City habitat, dumps

D   Dunes and beaches

E   Evergreen groves

F   Freshwater: ponds, streams, reservoirs

M   Marshes, bogs, swamps

O   Ocean and ocean edge

S   Saltwater: harbors, bays, creeks

T   Tidal flats, sandbars

U   Uplands: fields, meadows, farms, golf courses, roadsides

W   Woodlands, forests

Species	Habitat	Jan.	Feb.	March	April	May	June	July	Aug.	Sept.	Oct.	Nov.	Dec.
Common Loon	F, O, S												
Red-throated Loon	O, S												
Red-necked Grebe	O, S												
Horned Grebe	O, S												
Pied-billed Grebe	F												
Cory's Shearwater	O												
Greater Shearwater	O												
Sooty Shearwater	O												
Wilson's Petrel	O												
Gannet	O												
Great Cormorant	O, S												
Double-crested Cormorant	F, O, S												
Great Blue Heron	F, M, S, T												
Green Heron	F, M, S, T												
Little Blue Heron	F, M, S, T												
Cattle Egret	U												
Common Egret	F, M, S, T												
Snowy Egret	F, M, S, T												
Louisiana Heron	M, S, T												
Black-crowned Night Heron	F, M, T, W												
Yellow-crowned Night Heron	F, M, T, W												
Least Bittern	M												
American Bittern	M												
Glossy Ibis	M, S												
Mute Swan	F, S												
Whistling Swan	F, S												
Canada Goose	F, S												
Brant	O, S												

Species	Habitat	Jan.	Feb.	March	April	May	June	July	Aug.	Sept.	Oct.	Nov.	Dec.
Snow Goose	O, S												
Blue Goose	S												
Mallard	F, M, S												
Black Duck	F, M, O, S												
Gadwall	F												
Pintail	F												
Green-winged Teal	F												
Blue-winged Teal	F												
European Widgeon	F												
American Widgeon	F, S												
Shoveler	F												
Wood Duck	F, W												
Redhead	F, S												
Ring-necked Duck	F, S												
Canvasback	F, S												
Greater Scaup	F, O, S												
Lesser Scaup	F, S												
Common Goldeneye	F, O, S												
Bufflehead	F, O, S												
Oldsquaw	O, S												
Harlequin Duck	O												
Common Eider	O												
King Eider	O												
White-winged Scoter	O, S												
Surf Scoter	O, S												
Common Scoter	O, S												
Ruddy Duck	F, O, S												
Hooded Merganser	F												

Species	Habitat	Jan.	Feb.	March	April	May	June	July	Aug.	Sept.	Oct.	Nov.	Dec.
Common Merganser	F												
Red-breasted Merganser	F, O, S												
Turkey Vulture	U, W												
Goshawk	W												
Sharp-shinned Hawk	A, B, W												
Cooper's Hawk	A, B, W												
Red-tailed Hawk	U, W												
Red-shouldered Hawk	U, W												
Broad-winged Hawk	W												
Rough-legged Hawk	M, U, W												
Bald Eagle	F, U, W												
Marsh Hawk	M, U												
Osprey	F, M, S												
Peregrine Falcon	C, D, W												
Pigeon Hawk	D, U, W												
Sparrow Hawk	A, U												
Ruffed Grouse	B, W												
Bobwhite	B, U, W												
Ring-necked Pheasant	A, B, U												
King Rail	M												
Clapper Rail	M												
Virginia Rail	M												
Sora	M												
Common Gallinule	F, M												
American Coot	F, S												
American Oystercatcher	D, T												
Semipalmated Plover	D, T												
Piping Plover	D												

Species	Habitat
Killdeer	F, U, T
American Golden Plover	U
Black-bellied Plover	D, M, T
Ruddy Turnstone	D, T
American Woodcock	B, M, U
Common Snipe	F, M
Whimbrel	M, T
Upland Plover	U
Spotted Sandpiper	F, S, T
Solitary Sandpiper	F, T
Willet	T
Greater Yellowlegs	F, M, S, T
Lesser Yellowlegs	M, T
Knot	M, T
Purple Sandpiper	S, O
Pectoral Sandpiper	M, T
White-rumped Sandpiper	M, T
Baird's Sandpiper	M, T
Least Sandpiper	F, M, T
Curlew Sandpiper	M, T
Dunlin	D, T
Short-billed Dowitcher,	M, T
Long-billed Dowitcher	T
Stilt Sandpiper	M, T
Semipalmated Sandpiper	D, M, T
Western Sandpiper	M, T
Buff-breasted Sandpiper	U
Marbled Godwit	T

Month columns (occurrence shown graphically): Jan., Feb., March, April, May, June, July, Aug., Sept., Oct., Nov., Dec.

Species	Habitat	Jan.	Feb.	March	April	May	June	July	Aug.	Sept.	Oct.	Nov.	Dec.
Hudsonian Godwit	T												
Sanderling	D, T												
Red Phalarope	O, S												
Wilson's Phalarope	O, S												
Northern Phalarope	O, S												
Pomarine Jaeger	O												
Parasitic Jaeger	O												
Glaucous Gull	C, D, F, S												
Iceland Gull	C, D, F, S												
Great Black-backed Gull	C, D, O, S												
Herring Gull	C, D, F, O, S												
Ring-billed Gull	C, D, F, O, S												
Black-headed Gull	S												
Laughing Gull	F, O, S												
Bonaparte's Gull	O, S												
Black-legged Kittiwake	O												
Forster's Tern	D, O, S												
Common Tern	D, O, S												
Roseate Tern	D, O, S												
Least Tern	D, O, S												
Royal Tern	D, O, S, T												
Caspian Tern	D, O, S, T												
Black Tern	F, M, S												
Black Skimmer	D, S, T												
Razorbill	O												
Thick-billed Murre	O												
Dovekie	O												
Rock Dove	A, C, D, U												

Species	Habitat	Jan.	Feb.	March	April	May	June	July	Aug.	Sept.	Oct.	Nov.	Dec.
Mourning Dove	A, B, U, W												
Yellow-billed Cuckoo	W												
Black-billed Cuckoo	W												
Barn Owl	A, C, E, W												
Screech Owl	A, W												
Great Horned Owl	E, W												
Snowy Owl	D, U												
Barred Owl	E, W												
Long-eared Owl	E, W						?	?					
Short-eared Owl	M, U												
Saw-whet Owl	D, E, W												
Whip-poor-will	W												
Common Nighthawk	C, W												
Chimney Swift	A, C												
Ruby-throated Hummingbird	A, B												
Belted Kingfisher	F, S												
Yellow-shafted Flicker	A, W												
Pileated Woodpecker	W												
Red-bellied Woodpecker	A, W												
Red-headed Woodpecker	A, W												
Yellow-bellied Sapsucker	A, W												
Hairy Woodpecker	A, W												
Downy Woodpecker	A, W												
Eastern Kingbird	A, B												
Western Kingbird	B												
Great Crested Flycatcher	W												
Eastern Phoebe	F, W												
Yellow-bellied Flycatcher	A												

Species	Habitat	Jan.	Feb.	March	April	May	June	July	Aug.	Sept.	Oct.	Nov.	Dec.
Acadian Flycatcher	W												
Traill's Flycatcher	F, W												
Least Flycatcher	A												
Eastern Wood Pewee	W												
Olive-sided Flycatcher	W												
Horned Lark	D, U												
Tree Swallow	D, F, M, S												
Bank Swallow	F												
Rough-winged Swallow	F												
Barn Swallow	D, F, U												
Cliff Swallow	F, U												
Purple Martin	A												
Blue Jay	A, B, E, W												
Common Crow	A, C, D, E, U, W												
Fish Crow	F, S, W												
Black-capped Chickadee	A, B, E, W												
Boreal Chickadee	E												
Tufted Titmouse	A, B, E, W												
White-breasted Nuthatch	A, B, W												
Red-breasted Nuthatch	A, B, E, W												
Brown Creeper	W												
House Wren	A, B, W												
Winter Wren	B												
Carolina Wren	B												
Long-billed Marsh Wren	M												
Short-billed Marsh Wren	M, U												
Mockingbird	A												
Catbird	A, B, W												

Species	Habitat	Jan.	Feb.	March	April	May	June	July	Aug.	Sept.	Oct.	Nov.	Dec.
Brown Thrasher	A, B, U, W												
Robin	A, B, E, U, W												
Wood Thrush	W												
Hermit Thrush	W												
Swainson's Thrush	W												
Gray-cheeked Thrush	W												
Veery	A, B, U												
Eastern Bluebird	A, B, U												
Blue-gray Gnatcatcher	A, W												
Golden-crowned Kinglet	A, B, E, W												
Ruby-crowned Kinglet	A, B, W												
Water Pipit	U												
Cedar Waxwing	A, W												
Northern Shrike	A, W												
Loggerhead Shrike	A, U												
Starling	A, U												
White-eyed Vireo	A, C, D, W												
Yellow-throated Vireo	A, W												
Solitary Vireo	A, W												
Red-eyed Vireo	A, W												
Philadelphia Vireo	A, W												
Warbling Vireo	A, W												
Black-and-white Warbler	A, E, W												
Prothonotary Warbler	A, W												
Worm-eating Warbler	A, W												
Golden-winged Warbler	A, W												
Blue-winged Warbler	A, B, W												
Tennessee Warbler	A, B, W												

Species	Habitat	Jan.	Feb.	March	April	May	June	July	Aug.	Sept.	Oct.	Nov.	Dec.
Orange-crowned Warbler	B												
Nashville Warbler	A, B, W							?					
Parula Warbler	A, B, W												
Yellow Warbler	A, B												
Magnolia Warbler	A, B, W												
Cape May Warbler	A, B, W												
Black-throated Blue Warbler	A, B, W												
Myrtle Warbler	A, B, W												
Black-throated Green Warbler	A, B, E, W												
Cerulean Warbler	W												
Blackburnian Warbler	A, B, E, W												
Chestnut-sided Warbler	A, B, W												
Bay-breasted Warbler	W												
Blackpoll Warbler	A, W												
Pine Warbler	E												
Prairie Warbler	A, B												
Palm Warbler	A, B, U, W												
Ovenbird	W												
Northern Waterthrush	F, W							?					
Louisiana Waterthrush	F, W												
Kentucky Warbler	A, W												
Connecticut Warbler	A, B, W												
Mourning Warbler	A, B, W												
Yellowthroat	A, B												
Yellow-breasted Chat	B, U												
Hooded Warbler	W												
Wilson's Warbler	A, B, W												
Canada Warbler	A, B, W												

Species	Habitat	Jan.	Feb.	March	April	May	June	July	Aug.	Sept.	Oct.	Nov.	Dec.
American Redstart	A, B, W												
House Sparrow	A, B, C, D, U												
Bobolink	U												
Eastern Meadowlark	U												
Red-winged Blackbird	A, E, M, U												
Orchard Oriole	A												
Baltimore Oriole	A												
Rusty Blackbird	F												
Common Grackle	A, E, M, U												
Brown-headed Cowbird	A, B, C, U												
Scarlet Tanager	A, B, W												
Summer Tanager	A, W												
Cardinal	A, B												
Rose-breasted Grosbeak	A, B, W												
Blue Grosbeak	A, B												
Indigo Bunting	A, B, U												
Dickcissel	A, B, U												
Evening Grosbeak	A, E												
Purple Finch	A, E, W												
House Finch	A, E												
Pine Grosbeak	E, W												
Common Redpoll	A, B												
Pine Siskin	A, E												
American Goldfinch	A, B, W												
Red Crossbill	E												
White-winged Crossbill	E												
Rufous-sided Towhee	A, B, W												
Ipswich Sparrow	D												

Species	Habitat	Jan.	Feb.	March	April	May	June	July	Aug.	Sept.	Oct.	Nov.	Dec.
Savannah Sparrow	D, M, U												
Grasshopper Sparrow	U												
Henslow's Sparrow	M, U							?					
Sharp-tailed Sparrow	M												
Seaside Sparrow	M												
Vesper Sparrow	U												
Lark Sparrow	B, U												
Slate-colored Junco	A, B, E, U, W												
Tree Sparrow	A, B, U, W												
Chipping Sparrow	A, B, U												
Clay-colored Sparrow	A, D, U												
Field Sparrow	U												
White-crowned Sparrow	A, B												
White-throated Sparrow	A, B, W												
Fox Sparrow	A, B, W												
Lincoln's Sparrow	B												
Swamp Sparrow	F, M, S												
Song Sparrow	A, B, D, M, U												
Lapland Longspur	D, U												
Snow Bunting	D, U												

CALENDAR FOR A BIG LIST OF BIRDS

THE CALENDAR given here is a synthesis of many years experience by leading bird watchers and several field-trip chairmen of the Linnaean Society of New York. It suggests one field trip each week for centrally located watchers, with the over-all purpose of seeing as many different species as possible in a year around New York City. We must emphasize that dates and places are extremely *flexible* — that each week many other areas might be as rewarding or more so. In several instances we have included alternate places outside our area which should be particularly productive, if one can find it possible to visit them close to the dates specified.

January	7	Atlantic Beach and Point Lookout
	14	Pelham Bay Park
	21	Waterfowl count, a local area
	28	Montauk Area
February	3	Smithtown Area
	10	Point Pleasant and Shark River, New Jersey
	17	Jones Beach and Point Lookout
	24	Heckscher State Park and Carman's River
March	3	Bronx and Van Cortlandt Parks
	10	Croton Point
	17	Hempstead Lake Area
	24	Playland Lake and Rye Area
	31	Jamaica Bay and Riis Park
April	7	Lower Bay (Sewers)
	14	Prospect Park (or local woodlands)
	21	Lawrence Marsh and Atlantic Beach
	28	Mill Neck and Oyster Bay
May	4	Troy Meadows, New Jersey
	11	Bronx and Van Cortlandt Parks, or Jamaica Bay
	18	BIG DAY (visit a variety of areas)
	25	Rockland County
June	2	Pelagic trip (offshore)
	9	Grassy Sprain Ridge and Elmsford Ridge

June 16 Dutchess County. *Alternate:* Cape May and Fortescue, New Jersey
   23 Slide Mountain, New York
   30 Mianus River Gorge and Poundridge Reservation

July 7 Breeding-bird census, a local area
   14 Breeding-bird census, a local area
   21 Shinnecock and Mecox Bays
   28 Jamaica Bay or John F. Kennedy Sanctuary

August 3 Fire Island and Quogue Area
   10 Moriches Inlet. *Alternate:* Monomoy, Massachusetts
   17 Jones Beach and John F. Kennedy Sanctuary
   24 Hackensack Marshes, New Jersey, or a shore area
   31 Local shore area. *Alternate:* Brigantine National Wildlife Refuge, New Jersey

September 7 Pelagic trip
   14 BIG DAY
   21 Jamaica Bay and Riis Park
   28 Jones Beach and John F. Kennedy Sanctuary

October 5 Bronx and Van Cortlandt Parks
   12 Jones Beach, Jamaica Bay, or a hawk watch
   19 Jamaica Bay or Jones Beach
   26 Local hawk lookout. *Alternate:* Hawk Mountain, Drehersville, Pennsylvania

November 2 Lawrence Marsh and Atlantic Beach
   9 Heckscher State Park and Carman's River
   16 Staten Island
   23 Jamaica Bay and Riis Park
   30 Hempstead Lake and Rockville Centre

December 7 Orient Point. *Alternate:* Cape Ann, Massachusetts
   14 Playland Lake and Rye Area
   21 Christmas Count
   28 Christmas Count

FIGURE I. TYPES OF BIRD FEEDERS

A, suet feeder. B, feeder to be suspended from a branch or some other stationary
object. C, trolley feeder. D, suspended log feeder with holes for suet. E, weather-
vane feeder swiveled on a post so that it keeps facing away from the wind. F,
window-shelf feeder.

ATTRACTING BIRDS

Illustrations by Jane F. Pearsall

It is rarely necessary for bird watchers to leave their homes in order to see a variety of species. The smallest backyard will attract both resident and migrant birds, and when its natural conditions are improved by planting and supplemented with feeders, birdhouses, and other artificial devices its attendant bird population will be greatly increased.

Any bird watcher enjoys running up a good list of birds seen in his own bailiwick. A housewife gains pleasure from having birds visit her feeding stations, or the shrubbery close to her windows, where she may watch them as she goes about her household duties. Children, taught to observe the behavior of chickadees or woodpeckers on the windowsill feeder, find it fun to identify and point them out to parents and friends. Shut-ins and invalids discover a new world opening up for them when a birdhouse, feeder, or bird bath has been placed where they can watch it and pass the time without eyestrain or fatigue.

To attract and hold birds around the home, one must understand the basic requirements of a bird's life — shelter, food, water, and "housing" — and provide them under conditions as nearly natural as possible.

PLANTING FOR BIRDS

The dooryards most attractive to birds are those with an abundance of shrubbery, especially shrubbery that offers shelter and also produces food such as berries and other fruits. The presence, too, of garden plants that produce seeds almost certainly enhances the attractiveness. Most of the trees, shrubs, and vines recommended for attracting birds to dooryards will be found listed in several of the publications cited under "Sources of Information on Birds" at the back of this book.

It is always a good plan not to clean or tidy up gardens, dooryards, and hedgerows until winter is over. This leaves birds with many seeds for food as well as dead plant stalks for protection. If the hedgerows must be trimmed, put the removed twigs and branches in piles for shelters.

BIRD FEEDERS

Feeders may be anything from a simple windowsill shelf with a narrow edge around it to a large roofed-over structure, swiveled on a post with "weather vane" extensions to keep it facing away from the wind. A feeder that may be suspended from a wire or branch is often desirable. Some suggested feeders are shown in Figure 1.

Accessories for feeders may include a suet basket, seed hopper, and water dish. Sometimes it is better to hang a suet basket separately from a wire, clothesline, or tree branch, or to fasten it to a post or tree trunk.

When possible you should have several feeders. At least one should be stocked with bread and coarse grain for the more aggressive birds such as Blue Jays, Starlings, Common Grackles, and House Sparrows, and another with fine grain and seeds for chickadees, nuthatches, Cardinals, and Tree and Song Sparrows. Small dowels narrowly spaced between the roof and floor of a feeder will keep out the larger birds while admitting the smaller, but practically no arrangement will keep out House Sparrows without preventing entrance of the more desirable smaller birds.

Feeders should be placed not only where birds can find them easily but where they can be observed from the house and be conveniently serviced. Winter mornings that are bitterly cold and snowy are the very mornings when birds need food in good supply. If your feeders are close to the house — or better, within reach from a window — the more likely you are to keep them well stocked at such times. The arrangement is to your advantage as well as to the birds'.

During the late spring and in summer, birds are much less attracted to feeders because their natural food is in good supply. However, if you keep feeders in operation, a few of the permanent-resident birds in your neighborhood will continue to patronize them and, as the summer advances, will be followed to the feeders by their fledgling youngsters. You can then watch young Cardinals begging sunflower seeds from their parents even though they are able to crack their own, young Downy and Hairy Woodpeckers being stuffed with suet while they gurgle and yammer — these are rewards for your efforts in keeping the feeders going.

In the summer you can attract hummingbirds to your dooryard by having colorful, deep-throated flowers in your garden and by putting out hummingbird feeders. Simple-to-elaborate hummingbird feeders are available on the market, but you can make one from a plastic or glass pill vial that will do just as well. Twist some wire around the mouth of the vial, fasten it to a tall stick, and place it near some flowers which the hummingbirds are already frequenting. Put in the vial a solution of one part sugar and two parts water, or one part honey and three parts water. Then have some red color in evidence, because hummingbirds are quickly attracted to it. You can put red food-coloring in the solution, or paint the vial red, or tie a red ribbon around the mouth of the vial. Once the hummingbirds have discovered the solution and learned to drink it, you can place the vial anywhere and they will readily find it.

FOOD FOR FEEDING STATIONS

While numerous mixtures of wild-bird seed, all attractively packaged, can be bought at stores, you can stretch your bird-food budget by acquiring the necessary ingredients separately at considerably lower cost.

Birds such as Rufous-sided Towhees, Tree Sparrows, White-throated Sparrows, and Song Sparrows like finely cracked corn, obtainable from any feed store in 25-, 50-, or 100-pound bags at a reasonable price. The so-called "chick cracked corn" is preferable to "chick scratch," because the latter contains other seeds which most wild birds will not accept.

Chickadees prefer sunflower seeds, as do nuthatches, Cardinals, and Evening Grosbeaks. Sunflower seeds are expensive, especially when bought in small quantities. They are much cheaper in 50- or 100-pound bags. If you do not need such a large quantity, persuade some of your neighbors who have feeding stations to join you in purchasing and sharing a large bag. When possible, buy the smaller sunflower seeds. Though the size makes no difference to the birds, the smaller last longer and have more meat per pound than the larger.

Robins, Catbirds, and the occasional Mockingbird that may be in your area are particularly attracted to softened raisins, currants, and bits of chopped apple. Blue Jays enjoy bread crumbs. To bring woodpeckers to your feeding station you should always keep it supplied with suet. This will also bring chickadees and nuthatches, and an occasional Brown Creeper, kinglet, Myrtle Warbler, or Baltimore Oriole that happens to be wintering in your area. A large variety of birds like nutmeats (chopped peanuts or "Pecano"), peanut butter mixed with corn meal, and doughnuts (unsugared), cottage cheese, various dry cereals, pumpkin seeds, and meat scraps.

Some feeding-station proprietors make a "suet cake" consisting of melted fat, with corn meal, flour, and perhaps some sugar, raisins, nutmeats, and other foods stirred in. Seeds are not included, however, since the birds preferring suet cakes are not seed-eaters — and the seeds are only in the way.

BIRD BATHS

Birds that may never come to feeding stations will be attracted by bird baths. This is true even when there are streams and ponds nearby. An ideal arrangement is a *shallow* (one- to three-inches deep) basin with *roughened* surface into which water *drips* slowly from a leaking pail suspended over it, or from a garden hose, or from a fountain. The dripping serves to draw the bird's attention to the water, the shallowness of the basin permits the bird to wade into the water before bathing, and the roughened surface prevents the bird from slipping. The bird bath should be within a short distance of shrubbery, which will provide protection and perches. Although a bath is usually more acceptable on the ground where water belongs naturally, it may be elevated on a pedestal, post, or pipe, if it is likely to be disturbed or endangered by cats and dogs.

Some birds, such as hummingbirds, thrushes, warblers, orioles, tanagers, and grosbeaks, like to bathe under a light spray of water from the nozzle of a garden hose or a lawn sprinkler. When given the choice between a spray of water and a bird bath, they often prefer the former.

BIRDHOUSES

Birdhouses available on the market are infinite in variety and are frequently much more elaborate than they need to be. The general requirements for a birdhouse are: that it be made of wood, or perhaps roofing paper; that it be built to suit a particular species; that it be easily opened for cleaning; that it have adequate ventilation and drainage; and that it be properly placed.

The interior of a birdhouse should be deeper than it is wide, with the entrance hole near the top. A basic design for a birdhouse is shown in

DIMENSIONS FOR BIRDHOUSES

Species	Floor area (inches)	Depth of interior (inches)	Floor to entrance (inches)	Entrance diameter (inches)	Height above ground (feet)
Wood Duck	10 × 10	16–18	12–15	4	15–35
Sparrow Hawk	8 × 8	12–15	12	3	10–30
Screech Owl	8 × 10	12–15	9–12	3½	10–30
Yellow-shafted Flicker	7 × 7	16–18	12–16	2½	6–15
Hairy Woodpecker	6 × 6	12–15	9–12	1½	10–20
Downy Woodpecker	4 × 4	8–10	6–8	1¼	6–20
Great Crested Flycatcher	6 × 6	8–10	6–8	2	6–20
Tree Swallow	5 × 5	6	3–5	1½	6–15
Purple Martin	6 × 6*	6	1	2½	15–20
Black-capped Chickadee	4 × 4	8–10	6–8	1⅛	6–15
White-breasted Nuthatch	4 × 4	8–10	6–8	1½	12–20
House Wren	4 × 4	6–8	2–6	1⅛	6–15
Eastern Bluebird	5 × 5	8–9	6	1½	6–15

DIMENSIONS FOR NESTING SHELVES

Species	Floor area (inches)	Depth of interior (inches)	Floor to entrance (inches)	Entrance diameter (inches)	Height above ground (feet)
Eastern Phoebe	3 × 4	6	—	—	8–12
Robin	6 × 8	8	—	—	6–15

* Each compartment

Figure 2 and the dimensions to be used in adapting it to a particular species are given in the table on page 148. The top or roof should be hinged to permit access for cleaning. Two or three quarter-inch holes should be drilled in each side of the house under the edges of the roof so as to allow cross ventilation, and two or three more holes in the bottom for drainage. The house may go unpainted, since birds are more often attracted to one with a natural, weatherbeaten look. However, if you want to paint it, use an inconspicuous color such as brown or dark green.

Some variations in the basic design for a birdhouse are presented in Figure 3. House wrens will be attracted to almost any kind of a nesting device, but a house with an entrance in the form of a horizontal slot, one inch high by three inches long, is preferable (see Figure 3A). This prevents Starlings and House Sparrows from entering and facilitates nest-building by admitting the long grass stems and twigs that wrens commonly use.

A birdhouse should be cleaned out as soon as the young have fledged because it might become acceptable at once for the second or late nesting of another pair of birds belonging to the same or a different species. In any case, the house should be left where it is for the winter so that it may serve as a shelter and roost for woodpeckers, chickadees, or nuthatches. While

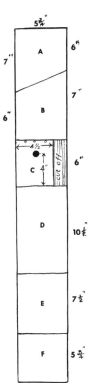

FIGURE 2. BASIC DESIGN FOR A BIRDHOUSE

The six parts of the house may be cut from a
1 × 6-inch board, 4 feet in length. See the
drawing at right. A and B, sides; C, front;
D, back; E, roof; F, bottom.

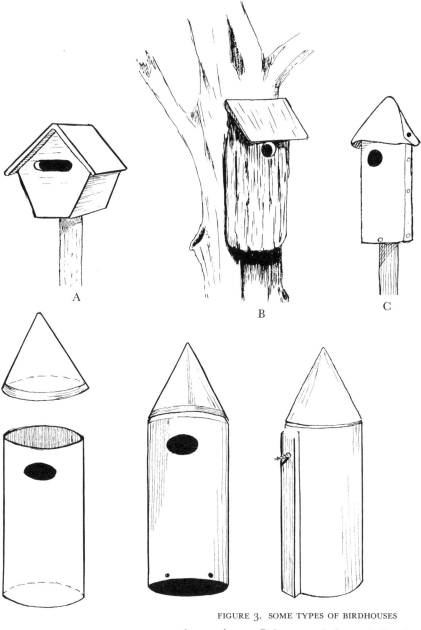

FIGURE 3. SOME TYPES OF BIRDHOUSES

A, wren house. B, house made from a hollow log.
C, house made from roofing paper; below, method
of constructing it.

it is usually considered advisable to empty the house of all contents in the fall, there is at least one good reason for delaying the cleaning job until March. Blowfly larvae, which cause the death of nestlings in a house, are in turn often parasitized by the larvae of the small chalcid fly. This insect may actually pass the winter in old nesting material. Consequently you may be aiding next year's nestlings if you refrain from removing the contents — and the chalcid fly — until March.

Although Robins and Eastern Phoebes will not nest in birdhouses, they will accept a nesting shelf (Figure 4), roofed over and open at the front, and placed under the overhanging eaves of a building.

FIGURE 4. A NESTING SHELF

Purple Martins, being a colonial species, require a house with several nesting compartments. Details for the construction of such a house are shown in Figure 5. The supporting pole should be hinged at the base so that the house can be lowered, and the house itself made in sections that can be easily separated to permit cleaning the compartments. The house should be painted white to reflect the sunlight and make it cooler inside.

Wood Ducks will accept several types of houses, provided their proportions are suitable. For details you should consult *Housing for Wood Ducks* by Frank C. Bellrose (Illinois Natural History Survey Circular 45, Urbana, 1955).

Placing a birdhouse properly to meet the habitat preferences of a species is just as important as building it to suit requirements. As a rule, it should be put on a pole by itself rather than on a tree, even though most species which accept any such man-made device normally nest in tree cavities. On a pole the chances of its being marauded by cats, squirrels, and other tree-climbers is reduced; and it can be further protected against climbers by a wide cuff of smooth sheet metal around the pole. The house should be set far enough away from trees and wires so that squirrels cannot reach it by jumping, and the base of the pole should be kept clear of shrubbery where predators might lurk. If the house is in a very open situation, the entrance

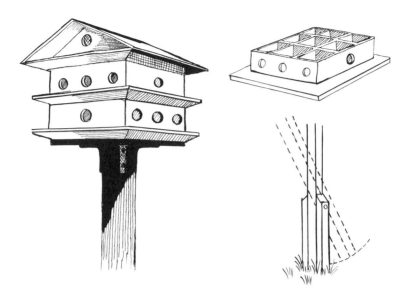

FIGURE 5. PURPLE MARTIN HOUSE
Details for the construction of one floor and supporting pole are shown at right.

hole should be faced away from the direction of the prevailing winds and usual storms.

Tree Swallows and Purple Martins prefer open areas, particularly near rivers, lakes, and ponds. Eastern Bluebirds also like open areas, but the presence of water is not a factor in selection. House Wrens are more readily attracted to dooryards and other semi-open places where there are scattered trees and shrubs. The forest-dwelling cavity nesters — woodpeckers, Great Crested Flycatchers, chickadees, and nuthatches — usually choose heavily shaded spots, occasionally woodland edges, and only rarely an open situation. Wood Ducks ordinarily nest near the rivers, lakes, or ponds that they frequent, but they will sometimes accept houses from several hundred feet to a quarter of a mile away.

Houses intended for Sparrow Hawks, Screech Owls, and Yellow-shafted Flickers should be placed some distance from dwellings on a tree trunk ten feet from the ground and not be painted. The inside of Flicker houses under the entrance hole should be roughened so that young may climb to the entrance more readily when the parents bring them food, and the bottom of the houses should be covered with coarse sawdust or shavings for nesting material.

LOCAL BIRD CLUBS

ANY BIRD WATCHER who wishes to increase his knowledge and skill, make the acquaintance of kindred spirits in his locality, and help support local conservation and education work is well advised to join one or more of the bird clubs active in the New York City area. Most of them have bulletins, all have worthwhile programs and field trips, and some maintain sanctuaries at various locations in our area. Bird clubs now active are:

Linnaean Society of New York, founded in 1878 and the nation's second oldest. Meets at the American Museum of Natural History (Manhattan) at 8 P.M. on the second and fourth Tuesdays, September–May, the third Tuesday of the summer months. Among its speakers has been almost every prominent ornithologist of this country.

Baldwin Bird Club, meets at the Baldwin Senior High School (Nassau) at 8 P.M. on the third Monday of every month except June, July, August, December.

Bedford Audubon Society, meets at the Bedford Hills Community House (Westchester) at 8:30 P.M. on the third Friday, September–May.

Brooklyn Bird Club, meets at the Brooklyn Institute of Arts and Sciences, Academy of Music, Arts and Sciences Room, at 8 P.M. on the first Thursday, October–May.

Edgar A. Mearns Bird Club, meets at the Washingtonville School Library (Orange County) at 8 P.M. on the first Monday, September–December and March–May.

Huntington Audubon Society, meets at the Huntington Public Library (Nassau) at 8 P.M. on the second Wednesday, September–June.

Lyman Langdon Audubon Society, meets at the Flower Hill School, Port Washington (Nassau), at 8:15 P.M. on the last Tuesday of September, November, January, March, and May.

Queens County Bird Club, meets at the Queens Botanical Gardens, Dahlia and Main Streets, Flushing, at 8 P.M. on the third Wednesday, September–June.

Ralph T. Waterman Bird Club, meets at the Arlington Junior High School, just north of Poughkeepsie (Dutchess County), at 8 P.M. on the fourth Monday, September–June.

Rockland Audubon Society, meets at Fellowship Hall, Clarkstown Reformed Church, West Nyack, at 8:15 P.M. on the first Friday, September–June.

Saw Mill River Audubon Society, meets in Pleasantville, Chappaqua, and Briarcliff, usually on the third Friday.

Scarsdale Audubon Society, meets at the Greenacres Elementary School, Huntington Avenue, Scarsdale (Westchester), 8 P.M. on the third Tuesday, September–May.

Section of Natural History, Staten Island Institute of Arts and Sciences, meets at the Institute in St. George at 8 P.M. on the fourth Saturday of every month.

At all meetings of the above-named clubs, interested visitors are always welcome.

There are also local clubs in nearby Connecticut and New Jersey.

THE FEDERATION OF NEW YORK STATE BIRD CLUBS, INC.

BIRD WATCHERS may also be interested in joining, as individual members, the Federation of New York State Bird Clubs, Inc. The Federation's stated objectives are "to further the study of bird life and disseminate knowledge thereof, to educate the public in the need of conserving natural resources, and to encourage the establishment and maintenance of sanctuaries and protected areas." In addition to meeting these objectives, the Federation is planning the eventual publication of a new book on the birds of the state.

Each year, usually on a weekend in the spring or fall, the Federation meets in a different part of the state with a carefully planned program that consists of field trips, a series of indoor talks and lectures (many illustrated), and a banquet addressed by a distinguished naturalist. Through these annual meetings, club and individual members have an opportunity to become acquainted.

One of the Federation's principal activities is publishing *The Kingbird,* a quarterly journal appearing in January, May, July, and October. Each issue contains not only original contributions to ornithology but seasonal summaries of the bird life and factors influencing it, written by Regional Editors, for each of ten areas into which the state has been divided. These Regional summaries are invaluable for information about the bird life in your region and for making comparisons of the migration or the nesting population from year to year.

Any person interested in birds should become a member of the Federation as well as join his local bird club. Not only will he meet many people with a similar interest and soon be better informed about birds in his state and how to enjoy them, but he will also be supporting, on a statewide level, the ornithological and conservation causes about which he is concerned. Membership in the Federation, including a subscription to *The Kingbird,* is $5.00 a year. Information about joining the Federation may be obtained from officers of your local bird club, or by writing the Laboratory of Ornithology at Cornell University.

BOBWHITE

SOURCES OF INFORMATION ON BIRDS

Publications on Birds of New York

Preliminary Annotated Checklist of New York State Birds by E. M. Reilly and K. C. Parkes. Albany: New York State Museum and Science Service [1959].

Birds of New York by Elon Howard Eaton. 2nd Ed. 2 Vols. Albany: New York State Museum, 1923. Out of print.

Birds around New York City: Where and When to Find Them by Allan D. Cruickshank. New York: American Museum of Natural History, 1942. Handbook Series No. 13. Out of print.

Birds of the New York [City] Area by John Bull. New York: Harper & Row, 1964.

Guides and Aids to Identification

A Field Guide to the Birds by Roger Tory Peterson. 2nd Rev. and Enlarged Ed. Boston: Houghton Mifflin Co., 1947.

Audubon Land Bird Guide (Eastern) by Richard H. Pough. New York: Doubleday & Co., 1946.

Audubon Water Bird Guide: Water, Game and Large Land Birds by Richard H. Pough. New York: Doubleday & Co., 1951.

How to Know the Birds: An Introduction to Bird Recognition by Roger Tory Peterson. Rev. Ed. Boston: Houghton Mifflin Co., 1962.

A Field Guide to Western Birds by Roger Tory Peterson. 2nd Ed. Boston: Houghton Mifflin Co., 1961. Useful for identifying accidentals.

A Field Guide to the Birds of Britain and Europe by Roger Tory Peterson, Guy Mountfort, and P. A. D. Hollom. 2nd Ed. Boston: Houghton Mifflin Co., 1966. Useful for identifying accidentals.

Birds of North America: A Guide to Field Identification by Chandler S. Robbins, Bertel Bruun, and Herbert S. Zim. New York: Golden Press, 1966.

Birds' Nests . . . An Identification Manual to the Nests of Birds of the United States East of the One Hundredth Meridian by Richard Headstrom. New York: Ives Washburn, Inc., 1949.

A Field Guide to Bird Songs. Two 12-inch phonograph records arranged to accompany, page by page, Peterson's *A Field Guide to the Birds.* Produced by the Laboratory of Ornithology, Cornell University. Boston: Houghton Mifflin Co.

A Guide to Bird Songs: Descriptions and Diagrams of the Songs and Singing Habits of Land Birds and Selected Species of Shore Birds by Aretas A. Saunders. Rev. Ed. Garden City, N.Y.: Doubleday & Co., 1951.

Books for the Study and Enjoyment of Birds

The Book of Bird Life: A Study of Birds in Their Native Haunts by Arthur A. Allen. 2nd Ed. New York: D. Van Nostrand Co., 1961. Student edition cheaper than trade edition.

Bird by Lois and Louis Darling. Boston: Houghton Mifflin Co., 1962. A book for bird watchers who wish to go beyond the identification stage.

A Guide to Bird Watching by Joseph J. Hickey. New York: Oxford University Press, 1943.

How to Watch Birds by Roger Barton. New York: McGraw-Hill Book Co., 1955.

A Guide to Bird Finding East of the Mississippi by Olin Sewall Pettingill, Jr. New York: Oxford University Press, 1951.

Song and Garden Birds of North America and *Water, Prey, and Game Birds of North America* by Alexander Wetmore and Others. Washington, D.C.: National Geographic Society, 1964 and 1965. Each volume is accompanied by a bird-sound record prepared by the Cornell Laboratory of Ornithology.

The Migrations of Birds by Jean Dorst. Boston: Houghton Mifflin Co., 1963.

Stalking Birds with Color Camera by Arthur A. Allen and Others. Washington, D.C.: National Geographic Society, 1961.

Pamphlets and Books about Attracting Birds

Attracting Birds by Waldo L. McAtee. Rev. Ed. U.S. Department of the Interior, Fish and Wildlife Service Conservation Bulletin 1 (1947). Obtain from Superintendent of Documents, Government Printing Office, Washington, D.C.

Inviting Bird Neighbors by Mary P. Sherwood and Eva L. Gordon. Cornell 4-H Club Bulletin 103 (1960, revised 1964). Available from the Cooperative Extension Service, New York State College of Agriculture, Cornell University, Ithaca.

How to Attract the Birds by Robert S. Lemmon. New York: American Garden Guild, Inc., and Doubleday & Co., Inc., 1947.

The New Handbook of Attracting Birds by Thomas P. McElroy, Jr. 2nd Ed. New York: Alfred A. Knopf, 1960.

Songbirds in Your Garden by John K. Terres. New York: Thomas Y. Crowell Co., 1953.

Homes for Birds by E. R. Kalmbach and W. L. McAtee. Rev. Ed. U.S. Department of the Interior, Fish and Wildlife Service Conservation Bulletin 14 (1957). Obtain from Superintendent of Documents, Government Printing Office, Washington, D.C.

Bird Houses, Baths and Feeding Shelters: How to Make and Where to Place Them by Edmund J. Sawyer. 4th Ed. Bloomfield Hills, Mich.: Cranbrook Institute of Science. Bulletin 1 (1944).

Books for the More Advanced Student of Birds

A Laboratory and Field Manual of Ornithology by Olin Sewall Pettingill, Jr. Minneapolis: Burgess Publishing Co., 1956.

Bird Study by Andrew J. Berger. New York: John Wiley & Sons, Inc., 1961.

The Life of Birds by Joel Carl Welty. Philadelphia: W. B. Saunders Co., 1962.

Check-List of North American Birds. Prepared by a committee of the American Ornithologists' Union. 5th Ed. (1957). (Order from the Treasurer, American Ornithologists' Union, Museum of Zoology, Louisiana State University, Baton Rouge.) This is the standard work for the established bird names, both scientific and common, the categories into which birds are classified, the sequence to be followed in listing birds, and so on.

Phonograph Records and Book Albums of Bird Songs

Records are 33⅓ rpm and have two sides. All are published by Houghton Mifflin Company, Boston.

Songbirds of America. Recordings of 24 familiar species accompanied by a book of full-color photographs and useful information on the habits and biology of birds. Produced by the Cornell Laboratory of Ornithology. Ten-inch record with commentary on both sides.

Bird Songs in Your Garden. Recordings of 25 of the best-known garden birds accompanied by a book of full-color photographs and information about attracting birds. On one side of the record the birds sing freely without the interruption of the human voice. Produced by the Cornell Laboratory of Ornithology. Ten-inch record.

American Bird Songs. Volume I. Recordings of 60 species. *American Bird Songs. Volume II.* Recordings of 51 species. Produced by the Cornell Laboratory of Ornithology. Each record 12-inch.

Warblers: Songs of Warblers of Eastern North America. Recordings of 400 songs of 38 warbler species. Produced by the Federation of Ontario Naturalists. Twelve-inch record.

Finches: Songs of Fringillidae of Eastern and Central North America. Recordings of about 400 songs of 43 species of finches, grosbeaks, sparrows, and buntings. Produced by the Federation of Ontario Naturalists. Twelve-inch record.

Journals on Birds

A subscription to the following publications is included in the dues to their sponsoring organizations.

The Auk (quarterly). American Ornithologists' Union. Dues $5.00. Robert M. Mengel, Editor, Museum of Natural History, University of Kansas, Lawrence 66045.

The Wilson Bulletin (quarterly). Wilson Ornithological Society. Dues $5.00. George A. Hall, Editor, Department of Chemistry, West Virginia University, Morgantown, West Virginia 26505.

Bird-Banding (quarterly). Northeastern Bird-Banding Association. Dues $5.00 E. Alexander Bergstrom, Editor, 37 Old Brook Road, West Hartford, Connecticut 16117.

Audubon Magazine (bimonthly). National Audubon Society. Dues $8.50. Les Line, Editor, National Audubon Society, 1130 Fifth Avenue, New York, New York 10028. Contains many articles on birds and regular sections devoted to attracting birds and bird finding.

Audubon Field Notes (bimonthly). A journal devoted to reporting the distribution, migration, and abundance of birds. Published by the National Audubon Society in collaboration with the United States Fish and Wildlife Service. Subscription $5.00. Order from National Audubon Society, 1130 Fifth Avenue, New York, New York 10028.

The Kingbird (quarterly). Federation of New York State Bird Clubs. Dues $5.00 (student dues $3.00). Dorothy W. McIlroy, Editor, 419 Triphammer Road, Ithaca, New York 14850.

THE CORNELL LABORATORY OF ORNITHOLOGY

THE CORNELL LABORATORY OF ORNITHOLOGY is a center for the study and cultural appreciation of birds, with headquarters in Sapsucker Woods, three miles from the main campus of Cornell University at Ithaca, New York. The Laboratory is open almost every day of the year and visitors are welcome whenever the building is open.

A separate department within the administrative complex of Cornell University, the Laboratory is primarily concerned with scientific and educational activities. For several years its research was conducted mainly in the fields of bird behavior and biological acoustics. Recently the Laboratory has broadened its research to include the following. (1) The aquisition, through field and laboratory observations and experiments, of any new information on life histories of bird species. (2) The acquisition, through the cooperation of many hundreds of observers in the United States and Canada, of statistical data on the nesting of all North American species, and the analysis of such data to determine population trends, rates of survival, and other phenomena. (3) Research on the ecology and distribution of birds, with emphasis on the controlling factors of the physical and biotic environment. (4) The study of local and worldwide migratory movements of birds at all seasons of the year.

An important part of the Laboratory's educational work is the production of motion-picture films and phonograph records of birds with matching color slides for use in schools and adult organizations. The Laboratory publishes an annual journal, *The Living Bird,* profusely illustrated in color and black and white, with articles and reports of interest to both bird watchers and scientists, and from time to time sponsors books and other publications by its staff and associates.

The Laboratory is essentially self-supporting, obtaining part of its funds for research and educational activities through the sale of phonograph records and record albums, matching color slides to accompany the records, and books and other printed materials.

The Laboratory offers two memberships.

SUPPORTING MEMBERSHIPS are open to all persons who wish to assist financially in the research, educational, and cultural programs of the Laboratory. Dues are $10.00 a year, payable at the time of application, and the first of each year thereafter. Each Supporting Member receives the *Newsletter* and *The Living Bird.*

ANNUAL PATRONSHIPS are open to all persons who are desirous of contributing substantially to the research, educational, and cultural programs of the Laboratory. Dues are a minimum of $100.00 a year, payable at the time of application and the first of each year thereafter. An Annual Patronship may be shared by husband and wife. Each Annual Patron, or the husband or wife sharing the Patronship, receives one subscription to the *Newsletter* and *The Living Bird* and one copy of such other publications as books, booklets, postcards, phonograph records, and record albums produced by the Laboratory during the calendar year.

For further information, price lists of records, slides, and publications, and membership applications, write to the Laboratory of Ornithology, Cornell University, 33 Sapsucker Woods Road, Ithaca, New York 14850.

ACKNOWLEDGMENTS

WE WISH to express our appreciation to the following artists for generosities, cooperation, and assistance: Orville O. Rice, for his bird drawings, eighty in all, that illustrate the section "Some Familiar Birds around New York City"; Jane F. Pearsall, for the drawings illustrating the section "Attracting Birds"; and William C. Dilger, for all the decorative drawings appearing elsewhere in the book.

In the preparation of the section "Where to Find Birds around New York City," the following persons have been particularly helpful in supplying information: Robert Augustine (central Westchester County), Robert Deed (Rockland County), John C. Dye (Orange County), Michael Gochfeld (Putnam County), Douglas Heilbrun (Richmond County), Eugene Mudge (northern Suffolk County), Dennis Puleston (information on Suffolk County), Gilbert Raynor (Suffolk County), Guy Tudor (information on the entire area), Otis Waterman (Dutchess County), and Sam Yeaton (northern Queens County). Other persons who also supplied information of great value were Irwin M. Alperin, Paul Baur, Ned Boyajian, John Bull, Geoffrey Carleton, Richard Chamberlain, Eleanor Dater, Scott Dearolf, Roy Latham, John H. Mayer, William Norse, John C. Orth, George A. Rose, Paul Stoutenburgh, and Audrey Wrede. The authors gleaned much useful information from articles in local bird club publications, brochures, and checklists, some of them by George W. Brack, Richard B. Fischer, Harry N. Darrow, Richard Ryan, and Edward D. Treacy.

The handsome maps in this book were the work of a committee of the Linnaean Society of New York, with whose permission they are published. They were originally prepared for a book that was to be similar to this one. Chief among the many persons who have devoted countless hours to the preparation of these maps are James Nolan and Richard Edes Harrison. Later, Mr. Harrison, aided by George Colbert, generously contributed revisions to the original Linnaean maps, and the map of Jamaica Bay Wildlife Refuge and several other original maps are published here with Mr. Harrison's special permission.

We recognize that the concept and title of this book are not original with us, having been suggested by the Michigan Audubon Society's *Enjoying Birds in Michigan* and later adapted to the Maine Audubon Society's *Enjoying Maine Birds*. We are grateful to both of these organizations for consenting to this current adaptation. Moreover, we wish to thank Alfred O. Gross, Howard L. Mendall, and Richard L. Zusi, three of the four authors of *Some Familiar Maine Birds* in the Maine booklet for letting us incorporate parts of their text in our section, "Some Familiar Birds around New York City."

In writing certain sections of this book we have also drawn on information from *A Guide to Bird Finding East of the Mississippi* by O. S. Pettingill, Jr. (New York: Oxford University Press, 1951), *Birds around New York City* by Allan D. Cruickshank (New York: American Museum of Natural History, 1942), and *Birds of the New York Area* by John L. Bull (New York: Harper & Row, 1964), as well as numerous other material such as brochures, booklets, and regional checklists.

Finally, for typing, editing, correcting, suggesting, questioning, and above all being patient, we owe a debt of everlasting gratitude to Renée (Mrs. Robert S.) Arbib.

THE AUTHORS

Index

INDEX

This is essentially a selective index to common names of individual bird species and place names. The boldface numbers indicate the main accounts of the eighty familiar birds to be found around New York City.

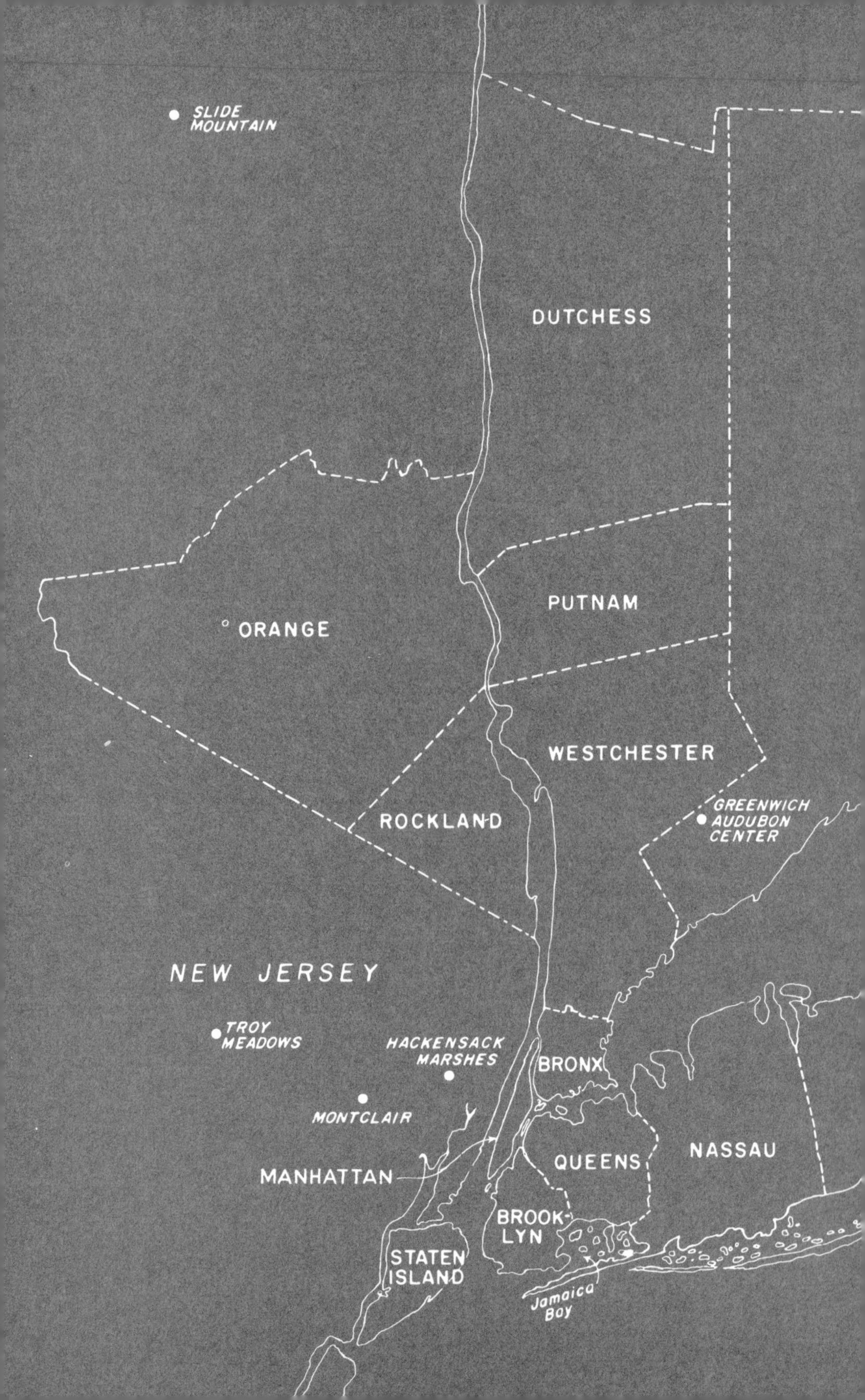
SLIDE MOUNTAIN
DUTCHESS
PUTNAM
ORANGE
WESTCHESTER
ROCKLAND
GREENWICH AUDUBON CENTER
NEW JERSEY
TROY MEADOWS
HACKENSACK MARSHES
BRONX
MONTCLAIR
MANHATTAN
QUEENS
NASSAU
BROOK-LYN
STATEN ISLAND
Jamaica Bay

AREA COVERED BY THIS BOOK
[see pages 55~124]

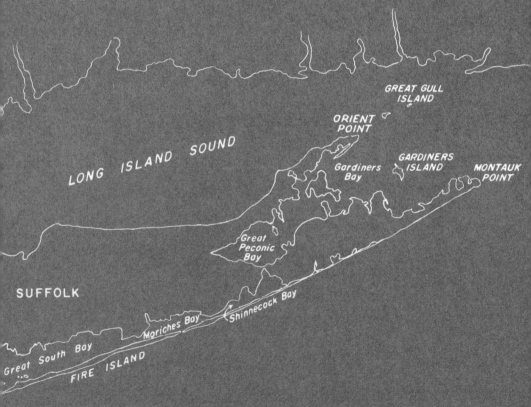

CONNECTICUT

GREAT GULL
ISLAND

ORIENT
POINT

LONG ISLAND SOUND

Gardiners
Bay

GARDINERS
ISLAND

MONTAUK
POINT

Great
Peconic
Bay

SUFFOLK

Shinnecock Bay

Moriches Bay

Great South Bay

FIRE ISLAND

ATLANTIC OCEAN